A LYRAN ALIEN'S GUIDE TO
ANIMAL COMMUNICATION

IO082280

BY SHEN THE LYRAN ALIEN

A LYRAN ALIEN'S GUIDE TO ANIMAL COMMUNICATION

By Shen the Lyran Alien

Galactic Skyrider Publishing belongs to
Cosmic Skyrider Ltd
5 Tal Building, Austin Road, Kowloon, HK

First Edition
Identifiers: ISBN 979-8-89379-201-0
Presented by www.lyran-light-academy.com

Galactic Skyrider Publishing

TO THE
ETERNAL
SOURCE

FOR HIM,
THE CENTER
OF MY EXISTENCE,
MY MECCA,
I WOULD NOT BE
WITHOUT YOU,
NEITHER WOULD
I HAVE COME,
FOR ALL TIMES
—ALWAYS.

THE LYRAN-ARCTURIAN FEDERATION, TOGETHER WITH SHEN'S SEEDER
CONSCIOUSNESS, RETURNED TO EARTH'S SOLAR SYSTEM IN OCTOBER 2021.

Contents

The Great Energetic Change:

Why you should Master Cosmic Animal Communication Now

The Story of Shen, the Lyran Alien

Shen's Message: The Future of Humanity as Intergalactic Species

Frequencies and the Matrix

How to use this Guide

The 1st Book

Chapter 0

Chapter 1

Understanding Different Realities, Dimensions and Viewpoints

Transform Yourself:

Spiritual Upgrades for Every Day to Support your Telepathic Communication

Mindfulness Meditation, Try Kriya Yoga,

Connect with Nature, Practice Empathy, Gratitude Journal,

Expand Knowledge, Reflect on Unity,

Silence the Ego, Serve Others, Karmic Entanglement, Limit

Materialism, Visualize Unity, Share Knowledge, Practice
Compassion, Celebrate Differences, Be Open-Minded, Set
Universal Intentions,

Foreword

ABOUT THE AUTHOR:

Born into Terran family, my early refusal to eat meat and harm animals was the seed that grew into a lifelong journey of compassion and spiritual exploration. This journey led me to learn from some of the world's most profound spiritual teachers, immerse myself in indigenous cultures, and retreat into deep reflection within Asian monasteries. Gifted with clairvoyance from childhood, my abilities to telepathically communicate with animals, engage with other-dimensional beings, and witness extraterrestrial entities set me on a unique path. These experiences nurtured my evolution into an artist, author of several books, a successful spiritual teacher, an acknowledged alien contactee, and a creator of innovative business ventures. I am a creative, multidimensional being, committed to shedding light on the universe's multifaceted truths. My work is dedicated to healing and enlightening, transforming the unseen into the visible and filling shadows with light. In this book, I channel Shen, my higher self and a member of the Lyran High Council, to bring forth the first telepathic guide for animal communication authored by a Lyran Alien. This guide is imbued with love, joy, and the profound connections that await between humans and the extraordinary beings among us.

This pioneering work is deeply enriched by the wisdom of Shen, a distinguished extraterrestrial from the Lyran High Council, recognized as seeder races and co-creators of the animal kingdom on Earth. The Lyrans, with their ancient and advanced understanding of the universe, feel a profound responsibility towards the beings they helped to create. This sense of guardianship is reflected in their role within the Galactic High Council, a coalition of advanced civilizations fostering peace, development, and cooperation across the stars. Shen, as an ambassador sent to Earth, embodies this commitment, offering guidance and facilitating a deeper communion between humans and animals. This book is not just a manual but an invitation to a transformative healing journey, encouraging you to remove the barriers to realizing your true self and to embrace your role as a "universal human." By fostering significant change starting with our animal companions, this connection promises to carve a unique path of love across the world.

Step forward with courage; your journey has already begun.

THE GREAT ENERGETIC CHANGE: WHY YOU SHOULD MASTER TELEPATHIC ANIMAL COMMUNICATION NOW

The transformation of the Western spiritual landscape marks the dawn of a new era, liberated from the higher echelons of reptilian dominance that once oversaw Earth. With their departure from our solar system, a new age of love and freedom emerges, beckoning humans to embrace their cosmic stewardship. This pivotal moment demands that we confront our fears, stand firm, and open our hearts to the harmony that exists among all beings on this planet. My book, "A Lyran Alien's Guide to Animal Communication," serves as a beacon for those eager to live in harmony with animals and otherworldly beings, dismantling the fears and prejudices that have shrouded our understanding for eons. The veil between humanity and the alien beings of this universe is lifting, urging us not to cower in fear but to embrace this revelation with open arms.

For those yearning to communicate with animals, to advocate on their behalf and to acknowledge them as multidimensional beings, this book is your gateway. Beyond animal communication, this guide offers insights into telepathic interactions with extraterrestrial life, a section you may explore at your discretion. I have always maintained that the essence of animal communication parallels the connection one might have with angelic entities. With the cosmic shift widening human perceptions, these foundational principles now extend to telepathic engagements with celestial beings and extraterrestrials.

Merging my human experience with my Lyran Alien Soul, I present "A Guide to Lyran Animal Communication." To my knowledge, this is the first extraterrestrial-authored guide dedicated to telepathic animal communication. The methodologies shared herein for connecting with animals are equally applicable to various extraterrestrial species. Shen, embodying my Lyran identity, intertwines humor with boundless love, creativity, and a zeal for imparting cosmic wisdom. This exchange aims to balance the energies between humans and animals, eradicating pain and suffering for all soul-based entities on Earth. You will uncover potent techniques and imagery codes to refine your advanced communication skills, fostering a secure and self-healing environment.

I welcome you to this extraordinary exploration of alien wisdom and, more significantly, to a deeper comprehension of animals. Let Shen ignite your child-like wonder, steering you toward enlightenment and cosmic understanding, and empowering you to champion animal rights on our beautiful planet. Shen's vision is to cease all forms of animal suffering and enslavement, equipping you with the knowledge to assist them. This empowerment enables animals to join the Federation of the Worlds as recognized species, ensuring their full protection and support as accredited members.

This is your awakening call. Embrace this moment, the very reason you're here and why this book has found its way into your hands.

MAY THE LIGHT FOREVER GUIDE AND PROTECT YOU.

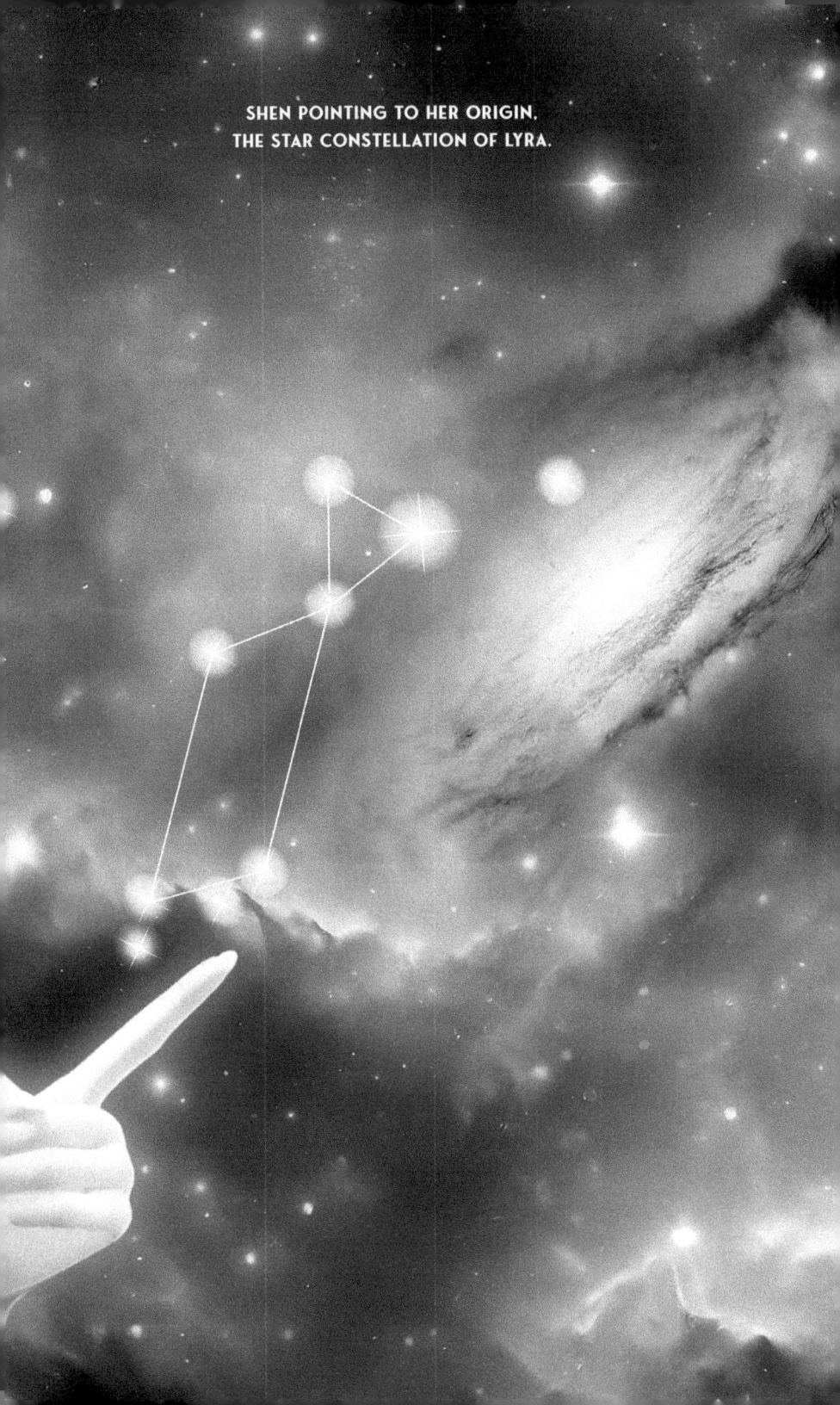

SHEN POINTING TO HER ORIGIN,
THE STAR CONSTELLATION OF LYRA.

The Story of Shen, the Lyran Alien

In our era, perceptions of aliens oscillate between malevolent perpetrators and benevolent messengers of light and love, with their intentions often perceived as revolving solely around humanity. Through my extensive interactions with various non-human, extra- and intraterrestrial species, I have come to understand that their existence transcends human recognition. They all share a common trait: a profound existence that isn't reliant on human acknowledgment. We must awaken to the reality that we are but a fragment of something vastly grander, and our greatest limitation lies in our reluctance to remember our true selves and to look beyond our narrow, earthly confines.

The emergence of UFOs and aliens in contemporary times shattered the human ego, which had been meticulously cultivated over millennia into a fortress of false self-assurance, perceived divine rights, and destructive capabilities like the hydrogen bomb. This paradigm shift occurred en masse, marking a significant evolution in human consciousness. Suddenly, humanity was no longer in its infantile stage; the Western world, in particular, had amassed power not only to annihilate itself but also to disrupt timelines and space continuums, thereby affecting the realities and well-being of other species across the universe. These encounters were not humanity's first brush with extraterrestrial life. Incidents like Roswell, the Washington flyovers, and numerous close encounters were merely awakenings from a deep slumber, challenging the once-unchallenged notion of human solitude in the universe and the resulting reckless aggression that even threatened Earth's well-being. Historic Figures like Oppenheimer and Einstein, having witnessed the terrifying potential of their creations, called for restraint and a reevaluation of our technological pursuits, recognizing our inadequate readiness to handle such power. We had unwittingly opened Pandora's Box, unleashing unforeseen consequences and revealing the "little grey enemy" at the bottom — a metaphor for the onset of modern alien awareness.

Human life, constrained within the brief journey from birth to death, often overlooks the eternal essence of our existence. Most individuals are ensnared in a perpetual state of fear — fear of poverty, loss of love, health, or death — which anchors our focus to the material, three-dimensional world. This paradigm, perpetuated by a reptilian alien hierarchy for millennia, keeps us preoccupied with the rigors of daily life — education, work, financial obligations, the pursuit of fleeting pleasures, and procreation — all while maintaining a narrow belief in a singular, physical existence and the need to draw energy from other living beings, particularly animals. This perspective, taught by those who seek to control, deems animals as subordinate species due to their different modes of communication, thereby justifying their exploitation and consumption under the guise of survival.

However, there are enlightened humans, intellectuals, and scientists who challenge these archaic beliefs, questioning the rationale behind continuing practices that are no longer necessary for survival, given our advancements and alternatives.

This calls into question the necessity of many modern comforts and conveniences that were absent during our ancestral days.

Turning our focus to the cosmos, specifically to the Lyran Aliens, we find beings who perceive themselves as integral parts of a vast web of life, interacting with myriad species, belief systems, and civilizations. Lyrans, inherently peaceful, do not pursue personal ambitions or callings as such concepts are alien to them. They used to coexist harmoniously within their star system, interacting with various species, including crossbreeds, and rarely venturing beyond Andromeda, their gateway to the universe. Despite their exploratory nature, which led them to establish colonies in different star systems and influence civilizations like the Pleiadians, Lyrans preferred a more introspective existence. The arrival of the Draco Reptilians, however, disrupted this tranquility, ushering in the great Lyran expansion.

The notion of a "dark force" overtaking the universe may sound like a trope from a science fiction saga, but the reality, in my belief, is a conflict between powers driven by either integrity or domination. Unfortunately, the Reptilians, an ancient species known for causing distress across universes, are inclined toward the latter. Their assault on the Lyran Systems set an unprecedented scale of destruction. Lyrans, primarily telepathic communicators operating at an exceptionally high frequency, found themselves at odds with the Reptilians, who used varied dialects and were less attuned to empathetic communication. This difference in communication led to catastrophic misunderstandings when the Reptilians entered Lyran space, ostensibly for resupply, but was misinterpreted due to linguistic barriers and differing protocols, leading to devastating conflict. Shen, a survivor of these harrowing events, stands tall and slender with a glistering pale complexion, having ascended to notable ranks within the Lyran High Council. She places little emphasis on titles or specific missions, instead focusing on generating vibrations of love and aiding humanity's evolution into a more aware, cosmic species. Shen advocates for a paradigm shift in human consciousness — to alleviate suffering on both individual and collective levels.

She urges us to see beyond our self-centered perspectives, to recognize animals not as mere companions or resources but as cosmic beings endowed with vibrant and profound souls.
Her vision is for humanity to engage in a dialogue not driven by utilitarian needs but from an extraterrestrial perspective that respects all forms of life.

Free from the constraints of fear, ego, and justifications for inflicting pain, Shen stands as an exemplary teacher and guide in learning to understand both animals and alien species. My hope is that you, the reader, will open your heart to her teachings, freeing yourself from the archaic notion of what might be right and allowing the true energies of our animal friends to shine through. Once you learn to embrace the language of Telepathic animal communication, you will feel differently about yourself and your life.

You will also feel differently about your purpose on this planet, Terra.

You will feel happy and loved, and love will be in your nature. Hope and gratitude will shine in everything you do, and there will also be a slight tingling of excitement and an eagerness in your heart to share your knowledge with others, which I encourage you to do. As I step aside, I allow Shen's consciousness to lead us on this transformative journey, filled with love and anticipation for a new era of understanding this wonderful beings we had previously known as animals.

Shen's Message:

THE FUTURE OF HUMANITY AS INTERGALACTIC SPECIES

I am Shen. A female Lyran alien and cosmic being, I observe humanity at a crucial juncture. For too long, humans have been fragmented by superficial differences — skin color, language, land of origin, and beliefs. Each acceptance of separation is a step away from understanding your collective essence. You, the Terrans, are inherently one, yet you are more easily swayed and controlled when divided.

When you only see yourself in one timeline, believe in one life, and perceive it in three-dimensional space, you try to make the most of the present moment. You don't care much about the consequences and pain you inflict on others; you want to be alive, enjoy, and have fun, which is totally fine as long as it corresponds with the highest good of the universe. If this is the case, you are always in balance with all forces which are naturally attuned to the frequency of universal harmony.

Know that every time you divert from your rightful path, which is aligned with this universal harmony and your soul, you feel the response of the universe as karma. You shoot off your course like a plane missing the right landing strip, creating chaos.

Karma is basically the energy that could not evolve into higher frequencies because of the diversion that was created at some point by missing your soul's plan and universal alignment. This way, it's easy to see why your life is maybe not feeling right, or you have the reoccurring thought that you are missing something, but you don't know what. You are not attuned to your highest self; you are living instead in chaos, the output of you created at some point. Where there is an output of energy, there is also an initial flame, an input. Let's refer to this input as "force" because it is energy that you initially created and directed. Disharmony and pain may result from improperly directed energetic input, and you may not feel like yourself in this life. You become the energy, the emotion, and thought patterns that return to you, cycling in a program that was misdirected from the beginning. When you allow yourself to deviate from your own path and become out of balance with the universe, you create a matrix prison, a program in which you operate. This is the opposite of free will and love, where it's hard for you to feel the true nature of animals, celestials, and other cosmic beings because all you want is help for yourself. In this state, you believe in your emotions and the anger, frustration, and fear because this is the program you run on. Imagine you're wearing VR goggles and all you do is play a game in which you try to escape a bad environment, such as a battlefield, but you can't progress because every choice you make returns you to the beginning. It's the same energy circle over and over again, and everything that enters now can only be experienced within this program; the frequency of celestials, aka angels, animals and other multidimensional beings, are also interpreted within this program. Your program to read this information and energies is very limited and not based on universal law and harmony. It is based on the emotional experiences you have shared with them, and it also adds an emotional hue to your spiritual experience and animal communication in the now that was not originally present. Knowing this is important because it influences how you perceive animals in telepathic communication. It's your program that works with the information perceived, and this program needs to be cleaned and updated, and aligned with your original mission on Earth. This is why I decided to come forward, to help animals to live rightly as free species on a planet where humans and extra and ultraterrestrials, as well as others, coexist already and now learn to see and accept each other for the first time.

From my perspective, I see that human survival instincts are often manipulated by fear, driven by a deep-seated need to belong to something known that feels secure and is possibly protective, like one's own tribe or society. In the coming years, humanity will learn that humans are a part of something much larger, and that there are beings and creators that are much more evolved but still loving and guiding. I can only hope that humanity learns to have the same attitude toward animals in order to help them find their voice, free them from slavery, and protect them until they can be heard, listened to, and respected through spiritual or technological evolution.

However, true awakening by remembering your cosmic origins will flood your incarnated self with empathy. This profound empathy, resonant with the frequency of love, aligns naturally with higher forms of communication like telepathy. It's important to realize that telepathy does not automatically entail empathy; many extraterrestrial species, devoid of emotional resonance, communicate telepathically.

Every soul vibrates with its unique frequency, contributing to a harmonious universal symphony. Imagine Robins singing in unison on a summer morning. Each bird's song is beautiful alone, but together, they create a symphony. Their voices carry frequencies that, when harmonized, form a new vibrational energy field, much like their intricately woven nests.

Frequencies and the Matrix

Various frequencies construct the energy layers within what I refer to as the "matrix" — the foundational energetic wave carrying the soul's essence into a program, perceptible also as sound to humans. This frequency enables beings to exist across both material and ethereal realms. Please keep in mind that I will be using the word Matrix frequently throughout this book, and it must always be seen and read in context with the information provided.

There is no universal meaning for this word, so please don't get confused.

Humans often confine language within their cultural and personal paradigms, influenced by heritage, upbringing, beliefs, and absorbed knowledge. This interpretation is intertwined with individual and universal structures of light — the essence of a being.

A challenge for humanity, as I perceive, is the overemphasis on the individual, overshadowing the soul's potential. This narrow focus frequently leads to a limited understanding of animals, which are viewed solely as physical entities serving human needs — a reductionist view that has historically been instilled to ensure societal structure and survival, but denies empathy for other species. Such a perspective justifies human-centric rights, often at the cost of other beings, a mindset prevalent across human cultures and a barrier to revealing benevolent extraterrestrial existence.

As Terrans, you must move beyond ego-driven fear to embrace love as the core of your existence. True extraterrestrials, or "ultradimensional beings" like myself, can manifest in your three-dimensional space temporarily, constrained by its limitations like the current lifespan of a human body. Animals, or "Ana Ham" as I understand them, are ultradimensional beings too, evolving on Earth under the guidance of ancient alien species, including the Lyrans and others.

Humans, the true Terrans, are a cosmic amalgamation, their DNA intricately woven from various creator species. This diverse genetic tapestry allows us, the benevolent creator species, to incarnate as humans when necessary. Being a Terran signifies a unique cosmic blend tailored for life on Earth. This understanding is key to realizing that all existence is a result of cosmic co-creation. Humans and animals were co-created by different creator species or seeder races, which overlook the creation process."Through my message, I urge you to embrace your galactic heritage, recognize the unity in diversity, and awaken to your true potential as part of the cosmic community.

You are part of the creator matrix and therefore you are able communicate on the frequencies that weave the matrix together.

How to use this Guide

In order to establish a deep connection with the Animal Species, your personal development, some energetic updates, and your healing are crucial parts. To make this as easy as possible for you, every chapter has an exercise section at the end where you find several energetically guided ways to dissolve limiting patterns in your personal matrix as well as establish new programs. This is done by mindful mediation, which you find at the end of this book in correspondence to each chapter exercise and Mantras. We wanted to provide you with a guide that you can use time and time again to forge new energetic paths for your mission to help the Ana Ham (Animal Species) be understood and respected on Terra. We invite you to visit us at www.lyran-light-academy.com to join our starseed online meditations, courses and seminars and to visit Our Online Shop www.vegan-cosmic-universe.com does offer a tailored selection of energetic fashion carrying the symbols of Celestials that you can wear to strengthen your connection as well as Symbolic Jewelry. Now, enjoy your journey and be blessed.

The Human Awakening

INTO AN INTERGALACTIC SPECIES

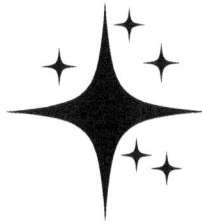

In the realm of multidimensional existence, every soul possesses its unique frequency and language, which contributes to a larger, harmonious symphony. This frequency serves as the foundational light that each creature's soul uses as a carrier wave for their language — an essential frequency if you will — creating existence on both the material and energetic levels.

When humans contemplate language, they often associate it with a specific tone, dialect, or wording that is accessible and comprehensible within their own understanding. This understanding is shaped by their cultural heritage, personal energy, social upbringing, values, belief systems, and the information they've absorbed. Furthermore, the complexity of their interpretation and comprehension is influenced by their genetics and the pathways through which they interpret and assimilate this frequency. Individual Frequencies are the fundamental (universal) structures of light that define the essence of the individual being, which transcends when fully integrated into what you call a person. The information or frequency that you use to structure your emotions and thoughts will be transformed into programs. You can also call them subconscious behavior patterns, code, the "way" you think or condition.

These programs allow you to act and become functional in the three-dimensional world.

They have little to do with the dimensional reality of the multiverse; they simply digest frequency within the emotion and images you allow them to. You use your life force and physical energy by creating and living this program. This is done by just living in what you feel is your normal everyday life or by updating, which starts with what is called spiritual awakening. Just living without creating spiritual updates in your life leaves you pretty much where you are in this and also in the next life. Hurtful experiences and emotions will form clusters that block the integration of new programs. The Hindu Celestials called them Karma. Spiritual updates using mantras, prayers, and meditation enable you to integrate new frequencies, neural connections, and light. By doing so, you will discover new programs and abilities and embody them in your incarnation. Additionally, you will become more connected to your soul's purpose and begin to break free from the reincarnation cycle, which will repeat the same emotions and mindset like a broken record player. What is outside of your program when you start to spiritually awaken cannot be comprehended at first. Therefore, new information and energies are mostly not accepted in the beginning; your mind simply blocks new information out. This is because there is a deep-rooted fear of losing what you have or what has been granted to you by the universe. Maybe you've had the feeling when someone, perhaps a Guru, says something meaningful to you that you can verbally and intellectually understand but can't integrate or process. Only after mediating with special Mantras and redirecting your program will the Guru's words make sense. This is one technique given to humanity by benevolent aliens and celestials, allowing you to work on your own programs and code them anew when your soul is ready. Sometimes, your mind is able to block new, positive frequencies off for years because it runs simply on basic survival mode.

For example, you like animals and believe they communicate telepathically, but you refuse to accept that they feel fear and pain in the same way you do. If you did, you'd have to eat a plant-based diet and avoid causing any pain to animals. By accepting only part of these beings, you will be able to understand only part of them. It's very simple because you let only a limited amount of frequencies through.

In my opinion, one of humanity's challenges is to shift focus from merely recognizing a creature's physical form and expressive abilities to acknowledging that each being possesses a soul.

Well, let's say, most of them and animals for certain. You have to transcend to an overall perspective that includes the recognition of the whole being in several dimensions, which is only possible by empathy and an open, loving approach of your heart.

This former tendency to judge by appearance leads to a high likelihood of perceiving animals primarily through their physical form. Through the lens of human survival or predominant needs, this form is observed and interpreted, resulting in descriptions of animal behavior patterns that may only convey survival, grooming, or herding patterns. The dogma of this perspective, of not truly connecting with these creatures, was ingrained in humanity long ago to establish a structured human slave civilization with a clear dominance hierarchy. It allowed humans to kill animals with less remorse. It simplifies matters for you, guiding you to concentrate solely on your survival and individual human needs. The denial of empathy toward other species and genders meant that you could secure the right to sustain and prosper primarily for yourself, your family, and your community. In later stages of civilization, this extended to your social structures and gods, ultimately culminating in the execution of your rights at the expense of the rights and lives of others. This behavior can be found in almost all human cultures and is one of the main reasons why benevolent extraterrestrial life is still kept hidden. Terrans have to leave their dominant behavior behind and choose balance and harmony as their sustaining force. They have to learn to live with each other instead of at each other's expense. Life beyond the four dimensions is not about survival; it's about coexistence simply because a lot of beings have very long lives, and some of them do not even exist in a physical body. Consider what would happen in your mind if you fully accepted eternal life and realized that the universe provides everything you need at the moment that you are able to accept and create without the fear of having too little or wanting more. Once you're ready, life on various frequencies, including multidimensional beings, animals, aliens, and celestials, will become visible to you. The universe teems with life, revealing itself fully when you embrace your eternal nature.

Understanding Telepathic

ANIMAL COMMUNICATION

"RECEIVING, SENDING, AND UNDERSTANDING FREQUENCY
PATTERNS BEYOND YOUR PHYSICAL SENSES IS A REMARKABLE
GIFT ENCODED IN YOUR DNA. ONCE EXPLAINED,
YOU WILL REMEMBER."
— SHEN

COMMUNICATION IS BASED ON THE EXCHANGE
OF INFORMATION THROUGH VARIOUS FORMS OF LIGHT.

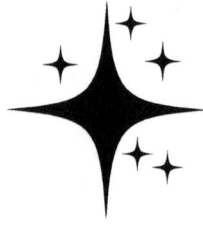

elepathic communication with animals, based on profound, unconditional love, transcends boundaries unlike human love, which often seems transactional—an 'I give, you give' arrangement from my perspective.

It's a love that comes with conditions, where love is received if certain prerequisites are met or if it aligns with human needs. This conditioning of love can often be traced back to your childhood experiences, where your survival was intricately tied to your mother's love. During those early years, you learned that specific behaviors were necessary to earn love and affection, essentially forming a "deal" or conditional love. If the criteria for your mother's love and attention, such as certain behaviors and appearances, were not met by you as a child, you might still feel insecure as an adult, believing that love must be earned and is based on exchange.

Lyrans, with their unique perspectives, understand that this conditioned approach to love can be a significant obstacle when trying to comprehend beings existing in different dimensions.

It can lead to misunderstandings and misinterpretations. For instance, if your fundamental concept of love is based on exchange, you might expect extraterrestrials to be either benevolent or malevolent, to act in your favor and love you, or to pose a threat. This is a human-centric approach. Most extraterrestrial beings have their own life experiences and worldviews. To transition into cosmic beings, you must accept that humanity is not the center point of the universe.

Individualism, the tendency to constantly place oneself at the center of all that occurs, is a human drama. It's akin to a child's approach to gaining love and attention, which can be understood in the context of human history, including millennia of perceived slavery under the reptilians. As you awaken to the awareness of a non-material world, often referred to as the spiritual realm, you naturally apply the similar logic, hierarchy and mirror the worldview you know from your material world.

UNDERSTANDING DIFFERENT REALITIES, DIMENSIONS AND VIEWPOINTS

In the vast expanse of the universe, uncountable different beings coexist, each rooted in their unique energy and consciousness. To maintain harmony, it's imperative to embrace mutual worldviews and assign equal value to other species as you do to yourselves. This means relinquishing your roles as the central figures in your individual dramas and dissolving your ego personas to rediscover your essence as beings of light, bridging the gap between your physical selves and your souls while eliminating the intermediary — your ego. Now, envision a world where animals think and feel like cosmic beings, for they are essentially extraterrestrials navigating your earthly realm.

To genuinely understand them, you must shift your perspective, shedding human-centric interpretations in favor of understanding the cosmic language of telepathy. In the not-so-distant future, you anticipate the development of AI programs capable of deciphering sound and ultrasound patterns accurately, allowing you to comprehend the spoken language of animals. These technologies will also extend to decoding gestures, much like members of the Cosmic Federation must understand non-verbal cues from extraterrestrial beings. The timeline for these advancements, approximately 15 years or less, may depend on your ability to find sustainable alternatives to animal-based food sources and products. By doing so, you signal the benevolent alien races that you are ready to accept other life forms as equal, thereby not proposing a danger any more to life which is not able or willing to defend itself against violence.

However, as long as you continue to consume animals, your subconscious mind may block your capacity to understand and empathize with them, thereby obstructing the development of such technologies. Nevertheless, we look forward to a future where simple translators, integrated into the collars of your animal companions or your mobile devices, facilitate basic communication with animals. This exciting prospect fills us with hope and anticipation.

As we embark on our cosmic journey of self-discovery and consciousness expansion, we recognize the need for straightforward measures rather than intricate spiritual practices to lay the groundwork for meaningful, secure conversations. You have to understand what love is from a cosmic viewpoint and dive into it.

TRANSFORM YOURSELF ──────────────
SPIRITUAL UPGRADES FOR EVERY DAY TO SUPPORT YOUR TELEPATHIC COMMUNICATION

Transforming your dimensional perspective and embracing a more expansive, universal outlook can be achieved through daily practices and shifts in awareness. Here are some exercises that you can incorporate into your daily lives to provide you with the needed love to change your energies forward to telepathic communication. Just pick one or more of these upgrade options; whatever feels good and doable to you on a daily basis will serve you best.

Mindfulness Meditation:
Engage in daily mindfulness meditation to cultivate self-awareness and presence. This practice helps you detach from ego-driven thoughts and opens the door to higher consciousness.
When you wake up, sit still, don't reach for your phone or distract yourself.
Breathe and start to feel who you are and how you want to feel this day.
Images of emotions and to-dos will appear, push them softly away like clouds into another space, and stay with the feeling you have. When this positive feeling becomes strong enough, reflect on how you will implement and use it during the day.

This is a simple way to transform the day in your favor.

Try Kriya Yoga

The roots of Kriya Yoga are found deep in the history of the Hindu Celestial teachings.

Krishna himself provided a simple but extremely powerful guideline on how to connect to the universal energy. In his own words, "Sit still and straight and breathe the same length out as in. When the breathing is connected, guide the energy and breath to your third eye. Feel a slight expansion and open it up."

Stay in there and repeat as often as you can.

Krishna is the 8th Avatar of Vishnu, a multidimensional celestial, so this advice on breath work comes from a really highly developed being and is a clear and simple guideline for breath work provided by what you can call a god-alien.

Connect with Nature:

Spend time in nature regularly. Observe the interconnectedness of all life forms, acknowledging that you are part of a greater cosmic ecosystem. Sit somewhere still and listen.

God will come to you in the form you are willing to accept at that moment.

Keep an open mind and embrace God completely.

Practice Empathy:

Extend empathy not only to fellow humans but to all living beings. Recognize the sentience and value of animals, plants, and even seemingly inanimate objects. Try to feel them rather than perceive them visually. What does their energy tell you? What kind of love frequency do they emit into their surroundings?

Try to read the information emanating by feeling rather than by looking at someone or something.

Gratitude Journal:
Keep a gratitude journal and daily record the things you are thankful for.
This practice shifts your focus from personal concerns to a broader appreciation of existence.

Expand Knowledge:
Dedicate time each day to learning about different cultures, philosophies, and cosmic perspectives. Reading, watching documentaries, and engaging in discussions can broaden your horizons. Don't leave this incarnation with the same knowledge you arrived with.

Reflect on Unity:
Contemplate the concept of unity in diversity. Recognize that diversity is an integral part of the cosmic tapestry and embrace it as a source of richness and learning.

Silence the Ego:
Practice recognizing and silencing your ego. When confronted with challenges or conflicts, consider how they fit into the grander cosmic scheme rather than centering them around personal concerns.

Serve Others:
Engage in acts of service or kindness toward others, human and non-human alike. Recognize that these acts contribute to the

universal balance and interconnectedness of all life. Kindness opens a lot of spiritual doors for you. It will slowly guide you to the ability to feel more love for yourself and others.

Karmic Entanglement:
Be aware that you have a lot of karmic entanglement going on. This is not specific to you; it's simply the result of existing in multiple dimensions as you do. Therefore, do not judge yourself and others too easily. Try to feel the connections you have and meditate if they no longer serve your highest goal, which should always be to exist in love and harmony as a cosmic being.
If they don't manage to do so for you, let them go or set new rules.

Limit Materialism:
Reduce your attachment to material possessions and consumerism. Understand that true abundance lies in the richness of experiences, connections, and cosmic awareness. You are already taking lots of stuff with you from one life to the other. Reflect carefully if what you have fills you with joy and love or weighs you down. If it's heavy and not needed anymore, sell it and give the outcome to charity. This way, the energy can dissolve in all dimensions.

Visualize Unity:
In your meditative practices, visualize the interconnectedness of all beings and dimensions. Picture yourself as part of a vast cosmic network of consciousness. One easy way for you to do so is to close your eyes and imagine the animal you are most connected to. Then, try to feel its parents, grandparents, and

so on, as well as all the guardians and guides who were with them. This is especially helpful if you do not have a lot of human connections.

Share Knowledge:

Share your insights and spiritual knowledge with others. Engage in conversations that encourage expanded awareness and mutual growth. It's not about fighting for your opinion, it's about the true sharing of everything that is magical and beautiful in this world. Keep in mind that if your human connections only share hate, anger, and jealousy, it's exactly the opposite of what you want.

Practice Compassion:

Develop a compassionate mindset, both toward yourself and others. Recognize that every being is on its unique cosmic journey. This does not start with a cat or dog. It's the bug on your window, the cashier you encounter in the supermarket, the cap driver. Everyone tries to live up to what he or she knows best. Try to recognize and encourage the light you can feel in someone but may not always see.

Celebrate Differences:

Embrace cultural diversity and appreciate the various ways in which different cultures and beings express their cosmic experiences. This includes culture on Earth as well as multidimensional, intra, and extraterrestrial cultures. Learn about these cultures and their values through useful and valuable information such as books by Dr. Michael Salla and others (see Discover Section).

Be Open-Minded:

Cultivate an open mind and be willing to challenge your preconceptions and belief systems. Explore different perspectives and be receptive to new Universal insights. Never believe that what you know is the final and only truth. Be ready for a daily update, for little wonders that can happen in your meditation, or for interesting news on a science blog you read. Not all information has to be useful in a material sense. But try to feed your soul with information that can be digested by your higher self and reintegrated in single and broken-down sparks when you need it. To be interested in only what serves you in the material world is reliving the reptilian mindset and acknowledging slavery, which allows only the things you need for your direct, physical survival.

MY NOTES

CHAPTER TWO

Clearing

YOUR EMOTIONAL PATHWAYS FOR TELEPHATIC COMMUNICATION

egin this process with the thought that maybe your reality is not as "real" as you think.

What if emotions and thoughts are simply a viewpoint pattern that you create in a specific time and space?

What if it is a program that helps you process the energies and experiences of that precise moment in your three-dimensional awareness of life?

Remember this idea and be aware of it. Your conscious mind will cover painful moments and override them in your mind in order to let you move on in your life. You crate emotions and opinions but not all of them are real. Your body instead will remember all emotions correctly as it is bound to bring your higher and lower senses into one experience. While we do this work, you may feel a certain itchiness, tingling, or nervousness in your body. Your mind may want to escape and do something else, like cleaning your windows or following any other distractions on social media. Remember that this is a way to avoid getting in contact with your real emotions which are connected to your body awareness. Have empathy for yourself and address the situation. Why is it so important to declutter your emotions? Because everything painful and buried in your subconscious, particularly your connection with animals, influences your telepathic communication with them. Unresolved pain will color what you send and receive with your higher senses.

Remind yourself that you have your higher self's guidance and love, as well as the spiritual tools I've provided you with to work with these emotions, transform and release them with love.

Now, reflect upon your relationships with animals throughout your life's journey. Recollect your childhood experiences and your emotions toward animals. Did you treat every being equally? Or were some considered insignificant, such as insects, which, interestingly, are the offspring of one of the most powerful alien races, the Mantis. Were you compelled to consume animals without fully comprehending its implications? Much of the shame, pain, or emotional blockages that hinder telepathic communication between humans and the Ana Ham beings originate from early childhood experiences.

During that time, choices were often limited, and you had to adhere to the perspectives and beliefs of your adult caretakers. Be compassionate with yourself and understand that your parents' and grandparents' generations were primarily focused on survival. They struggled to survive in a world where even human women and children had limited rights, and the Ana Ham beings had even fewer. Moreover, it was only in 2012 that the universe underwent significant changes in terms of power and the programs and possibilities provided by the matrix. Until then, the old matrix and its ideologies predominated the world power structure.

Terrans were unable to create their own light-based programs that could function above the fourth Dimension and its light structures. Let's say it wasn't impossible, but it took a lot of spiritual work over several lifetimes for a human to create this type of light matrix and remember it after rebirth.

It's important to grasp that some cultures were not governed by the reptilian alliance. Instead, they revered gods or avatars who provided a fundamental understanding of connections to the higher dimensions, and the humans who followed these ideals refrained from hunting or consuming animals from their early development stages as humans. Thus, even when they later encountered interference from other deities or occasionally resorted to animal consumption for survival, their connection to higher energy fields remained intact, as well as the connection to the spiritual realms of the Ana Ham.

In contrast, in Western civilizations, which were almost exclusively dominated by reptilian influences, such understanding was nearly impossible to attain. If you lived many lives in such dominant cultures, it's likely that this mindset and understanding have been passed down to you.

We observe that many humans inflict self-punishment due to a delayed realization of how they were treated in childhood for their love for animals. Some of you resisted consuming or harming your animal companions and where punished for it. We deeply empathize with those of you who witnessed the loss of a beloved animal friend only to be compelled to consume their flesh. Your emotions, boundaries, and universal love were not respected in these situations. Your empathy was not honored. Such experiences did create guilt in your subconscious, blocking a substantial part of your animal communication abilities. Instead of getting support for your love and empathy as a child, you where maybe mocked or neglected.

I'm here to assist you in acknowledging this guilt and transforming it back into the pure, unconditional love of a child. I'll also guide you in protecting these emotions so you no longer feel vulnerable during communication with your animal friends.

Once you've navigated the pain inflicted upon you by external circumstances, it's crucial to address any pain you may have caused yourself. Guilt is a significant impediment to telepathic communication. Additionally, it attracts entities that fuel your ego's defenses against confronting guilt. Some of you go to great lengths to block out entire situations because you cannot bear to face them. This can lead to intentionally or accidentally harming animals, such as through reckless driving, poisoning, or the destruction of species like spiders, worms, or any life forms unable to defend themselves on this planet against Terrans. Understand that these beings excel in self-preservation on other worlds and often possess intimidating sizes. What you perceive as an insect is maybe the remains of a former dominating species. Just because you encounter them in a small size now does not mean their energies are. Therefore, make friends, not enemies, by treating them respectfully. In certain animals like snakes, for example, higher beings like the Nagas, a very old extraterrestrial species with benevolence and malevolence, still tend to incarnate frequently. To kill or hurt a snake, therefore, can mean you make a mighty enemy in other dimensions, which will hunt you and your family for a long time, sometimes over generations. These and other beings can be very powerful when angered. Therefore, don't do so.

Guilt can also arise from decisions such as euthanizing a pet at the vet. A child's heart inherently knows right from wrong, but the guidance of adult caretakers often disregards these instincts. Socially accepted norms dictate how animals should be treated. However, there comes a point when you can no longer ignore your instincts, and your heart and intuition rise together and start to feel and realize the truth and another, higher reality. You will see that a lot of feelings and ideas you had as a child that were neglected or corrected by adults are pure and close to unity and love. I hope when you let this sink in and really feel it, you can regain your childhood purity. Then it will be very easy for you to feel animals and understand them correctly as they truly are.

CHAPTER THREE

Healing

CHILDHOOD WITNESSING OF ANIMAL ABUSE CENTER - CLEAR YOUR EMOTIONS

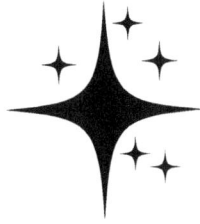

From a Lyran alien perspective, healing past traumas, especially those involving the suffering of animals, is essential for your personal growth and spiritual evolution. The exercises below are intended to help you overcome the pain and helplessness that come with witnessing animal abuse as a child.

BY DOING THESE, THE MEMORIES WILL NO LONGER INTERFERE WITH YOUR TELEPATHIC COMMUNICATION AND COLOR WHAT YOU RECEIVE WITH YOUR TRAUMATIC HUE.

PREPARATION:

Find a quiet and safe space.

Choose a quiet and safe environment where you can focus without distractions.

COMFORTABLE POSTURE:

Sit or lie down in a comfortable position.

Ensure that your body is relaxed and your mind is open to the healing process.

OPEN HEART AND MIND:

Approach this exercise with an open heart and mind.
Be ready to release past pain and find inner peace.

THE EXERCISE ———————————————
CLEANING YOUR HEART

1.) Relaxation: Begin by taking several deep breaths. Inhale deeply through your nose, allowing your abdomen to rise, and then exhale slowly through your mouth. With each breath, release tension and stress.

2.) Visualization of Healing Light: Close your eyes and visualize a warm, gentle, and soothing golden light surrounding you. Imagine this light as a healing energy that brings comfort and peace.

3.) Childhood Memory: In your mind, go back to the specific childhood memory of witnessing animal abuse.
Allow the memory to surface without judgment or fear. Welcome every image, even when it is painful or cruel.

4.) Observer Perspective: Imagine yourself as the observer of that memory, like a compassionate adult you are watching from a higher perspective. You are not reliving the experience but observing it from a place of safety.
What do you feel for the child having this experience, how can you help them, and what can you say or do to help the animal in that situation?

5.) Acknowledge Your Feelings: As you watch the memory unfold, acknowledge the emotions that arise within you. Recognize any pain, sadness, anger, or helplessness that you felt at that time. Do not suppress these emotions; let them come to the surface. Acknowledge your feelings.

6.) Healing Energy: Visualize a healing golden light extending from your adult self to your past self as a child. See this light enveloping your younger self with warmth and love.

7.) Comfort Your Younger Self: As the compassionate adult observer, speak to your younger self. Offer words of comfort, love, and reassurance. Let your younger self know that your animal friends are safe and protected now.
Comfort your younger self.

8.) Release Negative Emotions: In your visualization, watch as the golden light begins to dissolve the negative emotions, like pain associated with the memory. See them transforming into light and dissipating. Release these emotions, release the memory of pain. This does not mean you won't remember the animal the situation is about.

9.) Healing the Animals: Extend this healing light to the animals involved in the memory. Imagine them surrounded by the same warm, healing energy. Send them love and comfort, knowing that, from your higher perspective, you are making amends for the pain you witnessed. Heal them, whisper in their ear that you still love them and that you are sorry for what happened to them, that you were unable as a child to protect them.

10.) Forgiveness: Forgive yourself for any feelings of guilt or helplessness you may have carried. Understand that, as a child, you had limited control over the situation.

11.) Release and Let Go: With a sense of closure and healing, release the childhood memory and allow it to drift away, becoming smaller and less significant until it disappears entirely.

12.) Return to Awareness: Gradually return your awareness to the present moment. Open your eyes, take a few deep breaths, and feel the sense of relief and healing that has taken place.

13.) Be a Hero: If your self needs it, go back to the memory and be the Hero of your animal friend.
Create superpowers based on love, for example, golden rays, and protect your friend from any harm. Maybe you have to kick some human butts, too, this is totally fine.
It's not about being nice to everyone. It's about your connection with the animal and what you need to do in order to complete the experience and remove any emotional pain.

REFLECTION:

After completing this exercise, take some time to reflect on your experience.
Notice how you feel now compared to when you began.
Embrace the healing and forgiveness that has taken place within you.
Remember that healing is a process, and it may require repeated practice. The goal is to release the pain associated with past traumas and replace it with a sense of inner peace, compassion,

and self-forgiveness. From a Lyran perspective, this healing journey is a vital step toward your personal growth and cosmic understanding. You are not alone on this path, and the universe supports your healing and evolution.

MY NOTES

CHAPTER FOUR

Your Healing

IS PART OF THE JOURNEY

Next, we address the decluttering and healing of your emotional pain. When you carry pain, the Ana Ham beings can sense or read this energy, and they shy away. Most likely not in your practical daily life, there they may come to you and even try to comfort you.

But in a higher dimension, when they are not connected to your physical aura and energy field, they shy away when they feel pain. Fear and pain are read equally by Ana Ham, and if you carry this frequency because you did hurt one of them or you are a secondary carrier by eating meat, it still creates a vibrational distance. Basically, they fear certain aspects of you. This fear prevents trust and filters communication. The resulting gaps are filled by your mind with self-created emotions. Often, images of the animal's trauma and suffering are created which do not serve the animals healing and spiritual progress. You create this images based on your primary program which is the base program if you will. In this concept your brain does fill all "openings" that could draw you to self realization and to ultimate freedom with images that serve the overall concept of suffering, death and separation from love. In some cultures this is called Maya, a veil or curtain that separates you from reality while creating false images based on your fear and emotional needs. If you suddenly realize that you create pain and that this pain creates a distance between you and the ultimate source as well as animals, angels, celestials and so on, you could attain mastery of your own existence. This would imply that you have direct access to the source energy, or that you are free, multidimensional, and in love with everything that serves love only.

THE UNAVOIDABLE QUESTION: ARE ALIENS VEGANS?

The good ones, yes. The bad ones or races that are still in evolution, no.
But it's not about us or them; it's about you.
As you read this book, it's assumable you want to get clear and open-hearted telepathic communication with animals. The more love animals feel in all dimensions while conversing with you, the more they open up and show who they really are. Simply put, how can you expect to feel a cow's pain after eating a steak for lunch?

You inadvertently perpetuate the cycle of your own pain by consuming the animals.
Some humans argue that carnivores are animals that consume other animals in order to justify their ability to do so. However, this is not beneficial to spiritual growth. Animal carnivores have their own spiritual evolution which belongs to them. Also, you will find no higher-developed species in balance with the universe

that would do anything to inflict pain or suffering if it can be avoided. If you inflict pain, even on a secondary level, this pain energy is in your fields readable. Light energy instead, consumed over plants will allow you to develop a high frequency that does not frighten other beings. We Lyrans are light-based but have a plant-based origin far back in our history as we thrived in our own star system only. If you follow the idea that the humans as they are now were transferred from another planet or system — no it was not Lyra — where vegetables and fruit had a lot more energy, you can understand why it was important to condition them to meat eating. It was necessary to lower their frequencies. This way, it is much more difficult for a human to build up higher energies, get in full contact with its own soul, and communicate with celestials and benevolent aliens. When you are full of pain as a result of the food you eat, and you create more emotions in your mind through the way your programs perceive the world, your energy fields and receptors decrease. It's hard for you to feel and use your higher senses, like empathy. It is essential to understand that some animals, as you call them, operate from a basis of creating fear when they are, for example, hunting. But you will watch the same Lion peacefully in a water hole when he is not hungry, respecting the other animals and doing no harm. There are a lot of rules and interactions humans use to justify their behavior toward animals. We see a lot of confusion here because you learned to accept the idea of hierarchy based on domination by aggression. Try to see that there are different spiritual evolutionary processes going on, let's say, between a cat and a mouse. Generally, cats hunt mice, but you will also see cats that protect mice, feed them, and adopt them. Every species has its own evolution going on, just as you do.

Then, of course, you are confused because you assume humans have developed from animals and you have learned to believe that hunting and killing or the survival of the fittest mode would be part of your human nature. It's only natural to do certain things out of tradition or heritage or to fight nature in order to survive. This is just another lie that was used by the dark forces to make their system work and to use you in order to install pain, to keep you in a chromatic cycle of suffering and karma.

Once, there were several different highly developed human races on this planet, most of them vegetarian or completely plant-based. All of them disappeared or were replaced by more aggressive human species, which developed into the modern human later. Ancient texts like the Pyramid texts describe another tribe of humans that lived before the last flood, so do the Vedic texts, and even Plato spoke of a race of humans that was different and lived at a time when there was no moon in the sky.

HIERARCHIES IN THE ANIMAL WORLD

There are human animal trainers who argue that animals operate within hierarchical structures, suggesting that dominance is simply part of their nature. This is not entirely accurate. While hierarchies exist, they still enable these beings to experience unconditional love for every member. Their leaders do not dominate out of helplessness, aggression, or anger but rather to protect their communities. Your human "horse whisperers" are sometimes the exact opposite. Some employ fear to break a horse's will, controlling this fear by establishing rules and so-called education. This behavior bears resemblance to the actions of your reptilian overlords. Just reflect on your childhood, social structure, and the way you feel now when you look around in most societies. It's a dominance hierarchy, not a system based on care and love in which you live.

Your mind constructs numerous reasons to justify such behaviors because these patterns have been ingrained for so long that you've come to accept them as beneficial, which they are not. Every time a being experiences fear, it severs its connection to the light. This holds true for animals, children, and adult humans alike. When you create fear in your animal friends, it will hinder your ability to perceive them as cosmic beings, entities with their own thoughts and emotions and evolutionary plan.

HEALING YOUR IDENTITY

Another emotion we address is the fear of losing one's identity. This fear arises from the belief that survival depends on the individual mind. However, the concept of individuality was introduced to separate you from universal oneness. The "me" mentality seeks external validation of its ideals, values, and principles. It is disheartening to witness, in some animal communication conducted by mediums or communicators, how the questioner's ego-driven mind is in favor of the conveyed answer. Such interactions often lack the genuine connection that arises from unconditional love.

It is essential to break free from this pattern. Begin by opening your heart and trusting your love, purifying it, and liberating your inner child from limitations. Shed the notion that you can love too much; it is a falsehood casting a dark cloud over the awakening of your higher consciousness.

UNDERSTANDING AND HEALING GRIEF

Returning to the topic of pain, the loss of an animal friend can be an agonizing experience for many human souls. Grief, stemming from the fact that your friend has embarked on another mission, can be overwhelming. For Lyran aliens, the concept of death exists as well, but it signifies a transition of the body and mission. We leave our memories within the matrix's mind-emotion matter layer for accessibility. Should we reincarnate within the same world, timeline, and dimension, this love and connection remains like a program. Even when we do not reincarnate, we retain access to these memories. Therefore, while the emotional connection associated with a particular body form may dissipate, the spiritual being itself remains intact, as we understand the body is merely a vessel.

For many of you, the belief in death prevails, and you seek signs and answers from communicators to get in touch with your departed animal loved ones. However, by doing so, you overlook the fact that if your connection was rooted in a higher dimensional love and acknowledgment, your animal friend remains with you. To comprehend this, you must shift your focus from the three-dimensional world and expand your consciousness across multiple dimensions. This happens primarily through your emotional body. Your emotional body enables you to perceive and feel the true nature of existence beyond the confines of the three-dimensional physical body.

We will guide you through rituals to clean and activate your emotional body. Keep in mind that you must relinquish ownership of your feelings and the body-based connection to the Ana Ham beings. Do not fixate on the body you once knew when thinking about a departed animal friend. For it was just an avatar for a fragment of its real self after all. Embrace it as a multidimensional being, beginning with the acceptance of yourself as multidimensional. Embark on a wondrous, love-filled journey of acceptance for the various states of consciousness when you work on your grief. Also, you may have been told in your world that it is not appreciated to grieve over the loss of an animal friend. Maybe you had to swallow and hide the emotion so they could never be transformed back to light and reintegrated. If this happens, the energy cannot be transformed back into your soul energies matrix connection grid, and basically, you are missing a piece of your life love experience. It is important to address this because if not healed, it can be an access point for dark energies, which will use your vulnerability and emotions. We advise you to grieve, be sad, cry, and do whatever you need to do for three days when your Ana Ham friend does finally depart from their body. Then again, pray and honor your spiritual connection on the 40th day after they left their body. This will help your friend to order all energies of his physical and energy bodies, and dissolve memories and pain of illnesses. Always remember the moments of love and learning you had together. There are special rituals you find at the end of the book that will help you process the energies of both your Ana Ham friend and yourself in times of grief. It did not feel right for me to place this ritual in the actual flow of the book, so that is why you find them at the end.

MY NOTES

MY NOTES

CHAPTER FIVE

Cultivating

EMPATHY AND COMPASSION FOR ANIMAL CONSCIOUSNESS

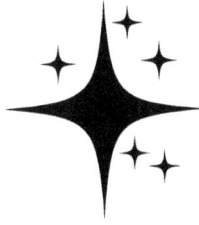

From a Lyran alien perspective, connecting with and understanding animal consciousness is an essential step in your cosmic evolution. This exercise is designed to help you cultivate empathy and compassion for the consciousness of animals and develop a deeper connection with them.

It's also important for you to really feel that the animal body form you are aware of is just one of many expressions of their energy.

PREPARATION:
Quiet Space.
Find a quiet and peaceful space where you won't be disturbed during the exercise.

COMFORTABLE SEATING:
Sit comfortably in a chair or on the floor with your back straight and your hands resting on your lap.

OPEN YOUR HEART AND MIND:
Approach this exercise with an open heart and mind, ready to embrace the wisdom of animal consciousness. Get into a child-

like emotional state, such as when you play with dolls or talk to a flower or ferry friend. Think of a time when you became so immersed in your world that you forgot about your surroundings and the passage of time

THE EXERCISE:

1. Centering Yourself:
Close your eyes and take a few deep breaths. Inhale slowly through your nose, allowing your abdomen to rise, and then exhale gently through your mouth. With each breath, let go of any tension or distractions.

2. Use the Lyran Connection:
In your mind's eye, visualize a radiant star filled with the energy of Lyran's consciousness. This star represents the wisdom and compassion of Lyran beings that will help you in your journey.

3. Imagine a Cosmic Web:
Envision a vast, interconnected cosmic web that connects all living beings in the universe. See this web as a shimmering network of light, with each point representing a unique consciousness.

4. Connect to Animal Consciousness:
Focus your attention on the part of the cosmic web that represents animal consciousness. Visualize it as a vibrant and intricate thread within the web.

5. Merge Your Consciousness:
As an observer surrounded by Lyran Energy, imagine yourself

gently merging your consciousness with the thread of animal consciousness. Feel the connection and unity between your awareness and the collective awareness of animals.

6. Experience Their World:
With your merged consciousness, allow yourself to experience the world from an animal's perspective. Feel their instincts, emotions, and sensory perceptions. Imagine what it's like to move, communicate, and interact as an animal.

7. Listen to Their Voices:
Within this merged state, listen carefully to the voices of animals. These voices may not be audible in the traditional sense, but rather a subtle understanding of their needs, emotions, and desires.

8. Cultivate Empathy:
Allow the feelings of empathy to flow through you. Feel the joys and challenges that animals experience in their lives. Embrace their vulnerabilities and strengths.

9. Share Your Love and Compassion:
As a human-terrain being, radiate love and compassion from your heart toward the collective consciousness of animals. Imagine this energy as a warm, healing light that surrounds and uplifts their existence.

10. Gratitude and Blessings:
Offer your gratitude and blessings to the animal kingdom for

their role in the cosmic tapestry of life. Recognize the wisdom they hold and the lessons they teach.

11. Return to Self:
Gradually disengage from the merged consciousness and return to your individual awareness. Feel the boundary between your consciousness and animal consciousness gently reestablishing itself.

12. Open Your Eyes:
When you are ready, open your eyes and return to the present moment. Take a few deep breaths to ground yourself.

13. When you have completed the first 12 steps and you feel a deep inner peace, warmth, and cosmic connection, you can do this exercise again but replace step 4 with the memory and love for animals. Keep completing the other steps as shown, and see what happens.

REFLECTION:

Take a moment to reflect on your experience. Notice any shifts in your perception of animals and your capacity for empathy and compassion. Consider how this exercise has deepened your connection to animal consciousness from a Lyran alien perspective.

Remember that this exercise can be repeated regularly to further enhance your empathy and compassion for the animal kingdom. By embracing the wisdom of Lyran consciousness, you are not only expanding your own awareness but also contributing to the harmony of the cosmic web of life.

MY NOTES

CHAPTER SIX

Telepathy

THE UNIVERSAL LANGUAGE

he universe is an immense space teeming with diverse life forms, including those we term "aliens" from a human perspective. "Alien" typically refers to life forms not originating from Earth, also known as extraterrestrial beings (ETs) or Extraterrestrial Biological Entities (EBEs). These aliens hail from specific regions within the universe, and comprehending their origins requires an understanding of the broader cosmic order.

In discussing the universe, we refer to galaxies, solar systems, and specific areas within them. It's crucial to recognize that the human concept of "space" primarily encompasses the three-dimensional, visible universe accessible to your perception. However, dimensions, densities, and timelines also constitute "space," where some aliens exist unseen by human standards. Additionally, concepts like time and light can be considered forms of habitat space.

In this vast expanse, myriad life forms exist, each with unique languages and communication methods. When extraterrestrials speak of humans, they refer to them as "Terrans," a term specifically used when addressing Earth's inhabitants. The universe hosts various humanoid species, each with differing moral alignments. Generally, these species are more evolved than Terrans, potentially due to ancient origins or the positive development of their planets, fostering spiritually advanced cultures.

A notable trait among these humanoids is telepathic communication, inherent in their genetic makeup. Humans possess a remnant of this ability, often experienced as intuition or a "gut feeling." This telepathic skill enables communication with many alien species and other life forms, like animals, and allows for simultaneous perception and understanding.

Aliens are categorized based on their regions of origin in the cosmos. When an alien enters a region different from its origin, it becomes an "alien" from the perspective of the inhabitants of that region. However, their species identity, such as "human," remains unchanged. This shift in perspective challenges human concepts of what is "strange" or "familiar." Humans often feel more connected to species that resemble them physically, such as the Nordic aliens, due to their humanoid appearance. In contrast, species with distinct appearances, like the Mantis Aliens or the Blue Avians (a tall, blue, feathery Lyran subspecies), might provoke discomfort or alienation because of their difference from familiar human forms.

Over the course of evolution, humans have experienced a significant diminishment in their higher senses, losing much of their spiritual awareness and becoming more reliant on physical senses. This reduction has intensified human tendencies toward preferring the familiar. This is evident in the diverse cultural practices on Earth regarding food, love, and religious ceremonies. Even within the human species, these differences can be profound. Acknowledging such diversity within humanity helps in understanding why extraterrestrial species in the cosmos do not share a universal language. Languages evolve based on the specific needs and communication abilities of a species within its particular environment, whether it's a culture, a solar system, or a community.

Some Terran languages, such as Arabic, Sumerian, pre-Egyptian, Hebrew, and, to some extent, Tibetan, are more widely understood by various alien races. This broader comprehension is not because these languages are exclusively Terran but because they incorporate elements of space, time, and specific frequencies that resonate with higher-dimensional meanings. Furthermore, telepathic communication surpasses traditional linguistic barriers, offering a more universal mode of interaction. In this context, different times and dimensions are navigated to access information from a universal source of knowledge, known as the Matrix or Akashic records.

WHY TELEPATHY IS THE BASE LANGUE COMMUNICATION MODEL OF THE UNIVERSE

Telepathy serves as a foundational language model for various entities, including aliens, interdimensional beings, and animals. Unlike conventional languages that are culturally and environmentally specific, telepathy is a more primordial form of communication. It's based on the direct transmission of thoughts, emotions, and intentions, bypassing linguistic structures entirely.

Communication Across Species and Dimensions: For alien and interdimensional species whose physical and cognitive structures may be vastly different from humans, telepathy offers a common ground for interaction. These beings might exist in realms where traditional sensory inputs and outputs (like speech and hearing) are irrelevant or non-existent. In such cases, telepathic communication becomes the most effective, or perhaps the only, means of interaction.

Natural Language for Animals: Animals that do not possess complex spoken languages inherently rely on a form of non-verbal, intuitive communication akin to telepathy. This allows them to convey basic needs, emotions, and social cues within and across species. Humans engaging in telepathic communication can tap into this natural language, fostering a deeper understanding and connection with the animal kingdom.

Efficient and Direct Communication: For beings operating on higher levels of consciousness or existing in different dimensions, telepathy allows for efficient and direct communication. It enables the exchange of complex ideas and concepts without the need for verbal translation. This is particularly useful in interstellar and interdimensional contexts, where entities might be communicating across vast physical or dimensional distances. Most UFOs are also bioengineered and interact telepathically with their captains on a conscious telepathic level.

Empathetic and Emotional Exchange: Telepathy often involves the exchange of emotional states and intentions, providing an empathetic understanding that goes beyond words. This aspect is vital in dealings with extraterrestrial or interdimensional entities, where emotional and psychological landscapes might be drastically different from human norms.

Subconscious and Higher Mind Access: Telepathy can access the subconscious and higher states of mind, realms that are often unexplored or underutilized in human experience. This aspect is particularly intriguing when considering interdimensional beings, who may operate primarily on these levels of consciousness.

Universal Cultural and Knowledge Exchange: Through telepathy, there is potential for a rich exchange of cultural insights and knowledge, transcending the barriers of language and physical limitations. This can lead to a profound understanding and learning between humans, aliens, interdimensional entities, and animals, fostering a universal exchange of ideas and experiences.

In summary, telepathy's role as a base language model is integral for communication across a spectrum of entities, including aliens, interdimensional beings, and animals. It provides a universal, intuitive, and empathetic platform for interaction, transcending the limitations of traditional spoken languages and enabling a deeper connection and understanding across various forms of consciousness. This is why I encourage you to acknowledge that Telepathic Communication is not limited to the Ana Ham Species. Instead, think of it as a universal language model that will help you understand and feel not only Animals, but also your other multidimensional incarnations, celestials, and certain alien tribes.

MY NOTES

MY NOTES

CHAPTER SEVEN

Telepathic

LANGUAGES OBSERVED IN TIME AND SPACE

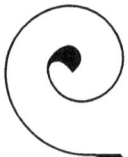

ow that we have discussed and clarified that telepathic communication is a widely used language, let me explain to you where this language can actually be used. Since we talk about a universal language, we have to start with the concept of the universe and how to perceive it when we want to understand this language in time and space.

To grasp the differences and relationships between concepts like the cosmos, universe, time, space, and realm, let's define each term and then explore how they interrelate:

Cosmos: The cosmos is the most encompassing term among these and is often used to refer to everything that exists — encompassing all of space, time, matter, energy, and the physical laws and constants that describe them. It is the broadest possible view of the totality of existence, including multiple universes.

Universe: The universe is a specific instance within the cosmos.

It refers to all of space and time and their contents, including planets, stars, galaxies, and all other forms of matter and energy. When we talk about the universe, we usually mean the observable universe, which is the portion of the universe that humans can in principle observe.

Time: Time is a fundamental part of the universe, often considered the fourth dimension in the fabric of space-time (the three spatial dimensions plus time). It allows for the sequencing of events from the past through the present to the future. Time is essential for understanding the evolution and history of the universe, from the Big Bang, which occurred (and still does) in multiple timelines to the present day. We Lyrans accept time only as a concept to navigate through different timelines, dimensions, and densities. Apart from this, everything that has happened, is happening, and all that you perceive will happen in the future is actually occurring in the now. Time is a navigational concept, not a reality.

Space: Space refers to the three-dimensional extent to which objects and events occur and have relative position and direction. It is often thought of in physical terms as the vast, seemingly infinite expanse in which all celestial bodies, like stars and galaxies, exist. In the concept of space-time, space is intrinsically linked to time as part of the fundamental structure of the universe.

Realm: The term "realm" can have several meanings, depending on the context. In a general sense, it can refer to a particular region or domain, either physical or conceptual. In scientific contexts, it might refer to a specific field or area of study (e.g., the realm of quantum physics). In more speculative discussions, such as those involving multiple dimensions or universes, a realm can refer to a distinct universe or dimension within the broader cosmos.

Please keep in mind that you will need these concepts to understand energy. Time does not exist as you know it; everything happens all at once, so you exist in multiple timelines, dimensions, and realities at the same time.

In order to move in this concept you have to agree on some sort of spacetime and directional concept. This also applies to spacetime and the use of wormholes, which can exist naturally or be created artificially and are known as stargates or portals. You have to agree on a space-time concept to direct your energy in order to interact with let's say an animal in a certain time of its life. Just imagine a movie you are watching. You can decide what story it is, what scene you tune it and finally when you interact and how. Watching the Matrix movies, Interstellar and Inception several times will help you to understand the concept.

COSMIC ORDER AND RELATIONSHIP

1. The cosmos is the all-encompassing reality that includes everything, even multiple universes and dimensions.
2. Within the cosmos, your universe is one specific manifestation, containing all the space and time you can observe or infer.

3. Time and space are interwoven aspects of each universe, creating the fabric of space-time in which events unfold, and objects and life forms exist.

4. Realms can be considered specific areas or dimensions within this structure, whether in a physical, conceptual, or spiritual sense. Think about the image of the earth being divided into different realms that belong to different alien or celestial species. This can be expressed by certain energetic protection or also affinities that are seen in the beings, both material and energetic, living in these realms. In short, every god or alien has its space (time), and humans usually reincarnate within the same realm because the energies or aspects of gods are their creator programs or holograms.

In summary, the cosmos is the broadest term and includes everything. Universes and multiverses are subsets of the cosmos, each with its own space-time continuum. Time and space are fundamental components of the universe, integral to its structure and function. Realms are specific areas or dimensions within or beyond your known universe.

All your telepathic communication with your Ana Ham takes place within this concept as long as you follow the reincarnation cycle in some dimension, time or density.

MY NOTES

CHAPTER EIGHT

Abuse

OF TELEPATHIC COMMUNICATION

elepathic communication, which transcends traditional language, plays a vital role in connecting humans not only with each other but also with animals, extraterrestrials, and multidimensional beings. This form of communication, relying on emotional exchange and mental imagery, offers a more holistic way of interacting than conventional speech.

Historically, human beings have primarily focused on survival within a three-dimensional existence, developing skills like hearing, speaking, and thinking, often at the expense of emotional and intuitive awareness. This has led to a tendency to suppress or misinterpret emotions, transforming them to conform to societal norms and ego-driven patterns.

However, telepathy, being a more direct form of communication, bypasses these distortions, allowing for a more genuine exchange of thoughts and feelings. It is important to know that several civilizations which you would call formally human and which are now far more enhanced, did loose their ability to use their physical senses. They evolved to be technically highly advanced and optimized for space and different environments. But with this evolution came also a price, the loss of senses, empathy, some spectrums of telepathic communication and they got infertile. Now, these races return from the future to merge with the current human race to update and rejuvenate their genes. Some of your humans are in contact with this beings which claim to come in peace. They promote hybridization and the blend of human and their aliens race.

Do not trust them; what is happening is not beneficial, and their actions completely oppose the Federation of the World, which views this movement as a subversive takeover of your world.

The Federation knows about their plans blending with humans into something which these Aliens do consider more worthy. Which basically means they plan to eliminate humans in favor of their own species over time.

I'm telling you this so you understand how important your feelings and senses are, and how they allow us to receive information that our physical senses cannot comprehend. Without them, you lose your connection to the light source and love, which is the sustaining force, and fall into the dark side, where pain and suppression reign.

Throughout history, there have been notable figures who have demonstrated an innate ability for telepathic communication, particularly with animals. For instance:

St. Francis of Assisi: Known for his deep connection with nature and animals, St. Francis has communicated with animals telepathically. Legends tell of him preaching to birds and taming a fierce wolf, suggesting a profound understanding and connection that transcends spoken language. St. Francis had a well-documented encounter with a UFO and aliens, which brooded his perception for all living beings and turned him into a vegetarian.

King Solomon: In religious and historical texts, King Solomon is renowned for his ability to communicate with animals and multidimensional entities, a testament to his extraordinary wisdom. This unique ability enabled him to engage with the natural world on a level far beyond that of ordinary humans. Additionally, he is said to have been in contact with the Djinn, an ancient race of beings that once ruled Earth before the reign of the Anunnaki. Djinn are known to possess both malevolent and benevolent traits.

King Solomon, attributed with possessing alien DNA, could understand the Djinn and even received a powerful ring from cosmic beings. This ring granted him the ability to control the Djinn and harness their formidable powers, which contributed to the construction of the first temple.

It's crucial to recognize that engaging in telepathic communication often leads to expanded capabilities, extending beyond interaction with animals. However, the direction in which you choose to focus your abilities is entirely up to you. I strongly recommend beginning with the safe and loving realm of the Ana Ham — your animal friends.

In contrast to human communication, many animal species and other entities utilize telepathy differently. For instance, most Reptilian Aliens exhibit a limited emotional range, predominantly centered on survival instincts such as fear or aggression. This characteristic hampers their comprehension of civilizations that are empathetic and communal. On the other hand, Tall White Aliens, who are also not amiable, possess a remarkable ability for telepathic communication and can access a person's emotions in their entirety. This capability renders them particularly perilous, as humans who have interacted with them often find themselves in a traumatic emotional state, their deepest connections to the universal emotional equilibrium disrupted.

As of 2020-21, there has been a shift in human consciousness, with an increasing number of people opening up to higher senses and embracing more universal forms of communication, such as telepathy. This shift requires moving beyond ego-centric perspectives, as the ego can distort the purity of telepathic communication.

Telepathy is essential in understanding diverse energy and thought patterns, which can be significantly different from one's own. It is a fundamental communication method within the

Federation of Worlds, allowing entities to embrace varied energy patterns without judgment.

Every human possesses the innate ability for telepathic communication, and it is part your genetic heritage. This ability encompasses connections with animals, extraterrestrials, and multidimensional beings. Indigenous cultures, along with historical figures such as Solomon and St. Francis, have exhibited this ability, often depicted within religious contexts that were established subsequently.

To engage in telepathic communication effectively, recognizing and embracing this innate capacity is crucial. It requires maintaining emotional purity and clarity to prevent manipulations or misunderstandings. Establishing one's identity and boundaries is essential to safeguard against abuse or deceit in telepathic interactions.

In summary, telepathy offers a powerful means of understanding and connecting with the cosmos and its diverse inhabitants. It requires responsibility, emotional clarity, and a willingness to move beyond ego-driven perceptions. By cultivating these qualities, humans can unlock their potential for cosmic communication, deepening their understanding of the universe and its myriad forms of life.

CHAPTER NINE

Telepathic

COMMUNICATION - THE CLARITY SELF TEST

etermining whether a communication is genuinely telepathic or influenced by one's own ego or external manipulation can be challenging. Here are three self-tests you can conduct to check if your communication is free of your Ego and negative Influences:

1. CONSISTENCY CHECK

Your Thoughts: When you receive telepathic communication, note its content and then divert your attention to another task or thought. Return to the telepathic message after some time and see if the content, tone, and emotional quality remain consistent.

Purpose: Genuine telepathic communication tends to maintain consistency in its message and emotional tone. If the message changes drastically or feels incongruent upon revisiting, it may be influenced by your own thoughts or external factors.

Indicators of Ego/External Influence: If you receive fluctuating messages, inconsistency in emotional tone, or messages that align too closely with your current emotional state or desires, it might suggest ego influence or external manipulation.

2. EMOTIONAL RESONANCE TEST

Your Emotions: Assess the emotional resonance of the telepathic message. Does it evoke a feeling of peace, clarity, and neutrality, or does it stir up intense emotions like fear, anger, or excessive excitement?

Purpose: True telepathic communication usually resonates with a sense of calm clarity and does not typically provoke extreme emotional reactions. It should feel separate from your emotional ebbs and flows.

Indicators of Ego/External Influence: If the message consistently triggers strong emotional reactions, particularly negative ones, or seems to feed into your fears, desires, or ego, it may not be genuine telepathy. Not every animal with an unlucky former life is traumatized. Not every abuse will be taken into the now and lived by the animal in endless emotional repetition. These are human emotional traits. Animals may exhibit dominant behaviors in response to negative events and may repeat these behaviors, but this does not necessarily mean they are deeply traumatized.

This is a general misbelief in human-animal communication and creates additional suffering for the animal. Sometimes, human-animal communicators unconsciously blend their own experiences of abuse with the emotions they receive from the animal. By reflecting these combined emotions back to their human guide, they inadvertently create a new emotional pattern in the matrix to which the animal must respond. This should be avoided as it creates suffering rather than facilitating healing.

3. ALIGNMENT WITH CORE VALUES TEST

Positive Message: Evaluate whether the telepathic message aligns with your core values and principles. Do the message encourage positive action, understanding, and growth, or does it lead to doubt, negativity, and destructive behaviors? Is there a victim and an abuser? If yes, check well if you accidentally touched the animal's human guide or your own story.

Purpose: Genuine telepathy should align with higher universal principles of well-being, growth, and positive interaction. It should not lead to actions or thoughts that are harmful to oneself or others.

Indicators of Ego/External Influence: Messages that encourage negative, harmful, or unethical actions or that cause you to act against your core values may be influenced by ego-driven thoughts or external manipulation. It's possible that you don't have the knowledge or emotional capability to help Ana Ham through a severe illness. You must be familiar with medications, how they work, and a variety of healing aids that can assist the human guide and animal doctors in understanding what the animal body wants and needs.

If this is not the case, a merciful death is practiced way too often in falsely interpreted communication that simply lacks information frequencies and practical knowledge from the animal communicator side. Be aware, and before you give a mercy kill advice, contact doctors, search the Internet, try to find answers, and create new information patterns. You would be surprised how easy it is to kill without knowing it because the ego wants to direct and give advice. There is also the problem with Human emotional endurance, since the humans have been directed to care only about themselves or their human family at best, there is a barrier when you're trying to really open up to be there for a creature form another species. You might want to turn your energy back to yourself because you have painfully learned over several lives that only your survival and that of your offspring counts. This idea plays heavily on the "one life only" thought. The inner pressure to end suffering is often nothing more than the wish to use all energy you have for yourself. There is no limitation in your energy, your are infinite so is the love given to you.

Self-Reflection: Regular introspection and meditation can help in distinguishing between one's inner voice and external influences.

Seeking Feedback: Sometimes, discussing your experiences with a trusted, objective person can provide additional clarity.

Gradual Development: Developing the skill to discern genuine telepathic communication from other influences often takes time and practice. Be patient with yourself in this process.

Remember, these tests are not foolproof but can serve as useful tools in your journey to understand and refine your telepathic abilities. The key is to approach this process with an open mind and a willingness to learn and grow. One of the best things to verify the quality of your communication is to practice with humans and discuss what you have received. This might be hard because of the feedback, which in the beginning is not always pleasant, but you will learn and adjust, like listening to radio waves. The most important thing is that you stay truthful about doing your telepathic communications based on love. The time will come, and the process will demonstrate the patients' love and understanding for themselves.

CHAPTER TEN

Your Unique

POWER TO COMMUNICATE

emember how you felt as a child, the way you perceived reality, and how you sensorially explored your surroundings, spaces, your parents, and animals. It was a profoundly direct and natural experience, wasn't it? You either made a connection, felt happiness as the energy flowed between you and the other person, or perhaps disliked someone when energy was not exchanged. You giggled out of happiness. You cared deeply about the energies and impact of words that you felt in the same moment as you heard the kindly spoken words. These fundamental emotions were the unrefined, primal aspects of your interactions. They were genuine. Options for engaging and experiencing emotions included crying, laughing, or just being curious about what would come next, leading to a smile, tears, or a neutral feeling. You either created a bond of flowing energy toward the situation or being, or you disconnected. Connection is communication at its core because every flow of energy carries signals and patterns, grids of information that your energy body unlocks and integrates. This process is dynamic and evolutionary, enabling you not just to transfer information linearly through time but also across multiple dimensions of space.

As multidimensional beings, your souls are propelled by the evolution of your interests and passions. From childhood, exploration is typically met with encouragement and affection, nurturing a feeling of achievement. Nonetheless, not all experiences are affirming. Punishment or neglect in reaction to a child's innate curiosity may foster fear and a hesitance to engage with the unknown, limiting one's emotional range.

Emotional understanding, crucial in children's development, is shaped by these early experiences. It involves recognizing, enduring, and organizing emotions, a process that influences how you perceive and interpret the emotions of others, including animals. Your personal emotional history can color your interactions, potentially leading to misinterpretation and distress in telepathic communication.

Revisiting and understanding your early emotional experiences is vital. It helps reshape your connections and avoid projecting your emotions onto others, like animals, ensuring more genuine and empathetic interactions. Without this introspection, your unresolved emotions may overshadow the true feelings of others, leading to misunderstanding and pain.

Now, think about your later childhood, from around four to six years of age. This is the time when your energetic aura body learns to sort and respond to energies, influencing how you perceive energy structures that are different from your own, such as animals, angels, and aliens when you sense their energy. If you felt the presence of a dark being under your bed, it is likely that one was indeed there. A "bogeyman" in your closet could have existed. Cold, foggy energy taking shape near your bed, touching your shoulder — yes, it could have been a part of the multidimensional species, sometimes intersecting with the human reality.

But what then? You probably told your parents about it because, in your world, they could make the bad things go away. This is a remnant from early human history when dealing with energies was left to the elders, your parents, or the tribe.

If the tribe and culture had encounters with angels and positive aliens, they had techniques for clearing or protecting themselves from negative energies. However, it's likely that your parents, particularly in Western societies, had forgotten this knowledge through reincarnation, or they themselves dismissed such experiences as a mere product of a child's imagination.

So, what did they do in your case, your childhood?
They reassured you that there was nothing there and told you to go back to bed.
Your conscious children's minds may have accepted these explanations. But your energetic self as well as your aura, belonging to a young and sensitive just incarnated being, was keenly perceptive to these energies. You just knew they were real, and over the years, assured by your parents, teachers, and

society, you just forgot about what was there and accepted these encounters as nightmares.

If you ever wonder why your movie portals and hubs are full of horror movies, this is why:

They give you an energetic and emotional framework to work with these energetic imprints. You think you can resolve this energy by seeing images and understanding this as part of Hollywood horror and filmmaking. But at night, when you may be unable to let go of these images and they are haunting you, you feel the energy behind them. I am not saying that all that's created in a horror movie is real and existing. But some of these ideas are very close to reality because somebody, a film writer, received this energy and made a story out of it. Behind the effects, the movie plot, and what else is going on, you feel the actual energy existing. Consider it the most immediate framework or program of which you are subconsciously aware of the unseen negative forces. This manifests as fear or haunts your imagination.

WHY MOST CHILDREN TRANSITION INTO 3-DIMENSIONAL REALITY BY THE AGE OF SIX

Many children on Earth find it challenging to transition into a three-dimensional understanding of life. This often leads to the neglect of certain energies, a natural response when there is no guiding "program" from the matrix to maintain awareness of a multidimensional reality. Such a program could have been developed by them in a previous or parallel life, or by elders, spiritual guides in their communities, or parents.

Without guidance on how to manage their energy flow while growing up, they end up blocking it through their chakras. This blockage impacts the development and expansion of their aura layers and their electromagnetic field. Consequently, their aura weakens, especially at the connection point to the higher bodies, and physical pain as well as emotional stress arises. These children learn to ignore these discomforts, feeling disconnected and sensing that something isn't quite right, a reminder that their system isn't functioning naturally. Also, fear is a very common side effect. An uncertainty of all that is felt but invisible to them.

Fast forward ten years to young adulthood. These early multidimensional experiences might be dismissed as childish or naive. However, when these individuals start exploring spirituality, they meet others who share similar experiences. They learn to constantly protect themselves, especially when they receive both telepathic and energetic communications. Unfortunately, without a fully functional energy body and a program to manage these energies, they can only process a limited amount of information. Most of these children have unknowingly built an energetic shield based on fear — fear of the unknown, rejection, and loneliness. This shield doesn't offer real protection but dulls the intensity of incoming energies. They still feel the pressure of the energy around them, like constantly pushing against a door from the inside to keep others' energies out. Their capacity to perceive is limited by this exertion, and their childhood program influences how they interpret these energies into emotions, information, and matter. If you share some of the experience, know that all of this can be corrected and healed in time. That is why celestials, benevolent aliens, and your guides show more openly now to help you overcome this fear and limitations with love and guidance.

CORRECTING CHILDHOOD FILTERS ──────────────

PLEASE READ THE FOLLOWING CAREFULLY AND FOCUS YOUR THOUGHT AND FEELING ON EACH SUBJECT:

CHILDHOOD ENERGETIC SHIELDS: Children often create protective energy shields, but these shields are built out of fear and limitations rather than love and understanding. This hinders their ability to discern and categorize different types of energies (positive, negative, and neutral). The ideal situation, which is rare, is for children to develop a strong shield from positive, loving energy, aiding them in better energy discernment. Don't worry, it's not great when you see yourself here, but it can be corrected with a little work.

PARENTAL ENERGY PROTECTION: Another method for children to protect themselves is by using their parents' energy. This is a natural support for the child's incoming soul. Unfortunately, it is rare in your Western society for children to receive this kind of energetic protection, therefore resulting in an awareness of positive and negative energies. You learn about what is wrong and right but not how to transform energies that are not ok into a healing stream of energy or light.

DIFFICULTY WITH NEGATIVE ENERGIES: Many people struggle with handling negative energies because they fear losing the little positive energy (light) they retained from childhood.

This fear impedes the development of a healthy approach to understanding and protecting against negative energies. All that could be negative follows a stereotype approach but no real teaching on how to read negative and positive energies. You can be tricked very easily by shapeshifters and others who live in your human societies, and this happens quite often.

TELEPATHIC ANIMAL COMMUNICATION: Remember that telepathic communication with animals is based on emotional frequencies of light. For effective telepathy, words, signs, or images are not enough; emotions, which carry energy, are crucial. Animals can't understand humans if their words are not aligned with their emotions. Native human tribes, who still possess this skill, communicate with animals not through word-based thoughts but through cohesive energy patterns of thoughts and emotions. They also use part of the Matrix to connect with the higher creational programs of some of the Ana Ham Tribes, like the Bear Tribe, which is often misinterpreted as "Group Soul." Some of your Terran animal communicators go so far as to say that animals do not have individual souls but only group souls, which is just wrong.

THREE-DIMENSIONAL COMMUNICATION LIMITATIONS: In the modern, three-dimensional world, people have become accustomed to communicating without incorporating energy, leading to a reliance on reading body language and facial expressions. This shift was deliberately engineered by "dark forces" to disrupt empathetic connections among individuals, enabling acts of hatred, pain, and cruelty. This strategy was a divide-and-conquer tactic employed by those in power.

HOW TO HEAL AND RECONNECT

From childhood, many people are taught to communicate with higher entities like God, angels, or celestial beings through prayer or via intermediaries. However, central to such communications is a powerful yet often overlooked aspect: your innate capacity for love and direct connection with the source. This boundless force serves as the universal medium for all your thoughts and emotions, transcending the need for external channels.

To effectively tap into your inherent power, it's important to reconnect with your inner child. This means revisiting and embracing the pure emotions you felt during your early years. These initial emotional experiences form the base code of our personal energy matrix — a critical system that helps translate and balance our energies, those of our higher self, and the energies of our environment.

By understanding and accessing this energy matrix, you can interact more directly and genuinely with the universe. This understanding aligns your energy fields with the dimensions you occupy, enabling a more profound and authentic cosmic connection. Therefore, reconnecting with the unfiltered emotional essence of your childhood can open new pathways of understanding and communication in your spiritual journey.

THE EFFECT OF YOUR SOCIAL CONDITIONING

Meditation and various practices can help reveal the limitations imposed on you, not by personal choice, but through societal conditioning. Healing your inner child and reforming how you establish emotional connections will enhance your ability to communicate with animals and other entities like Aliens. Be aware that Humans are known for their immense capacity for love, a trait believed to be inherited from an ancient, loving species that played a role in human evolution, and practically, when this force is fully integrated, you are almost limitless.

It's important to free this love from any restriction in order to extend your emotions to all animals, irrespective of their behavior, appearance, or reciprocation of affection. Learning to be emotionally limitless is key, and we, the Lyrans, are here to support you in this journey. As you develop the skill of communicating with animals, you'll experience personal liberation and become aware of the presence of guardian entities ready to assist you. Remember, animals should not be overwhelmed by human emotions, as they are still largely subjugated on Earth.

Reflect on the lives of domestic animals, like dogs, who are dependent on humans even for basic needs and may face harsh consequences for natural behaviors. As they age and their dependency increases, they often face severe outcomes. This reality creates a collective fear and anxiety among them. Until recently, we Lyrans could only offer our assistance at the end of their lives to beings interpreted by some psychic humans as angels, which also exist, of course. Some animal parents feel our support and help for our beloved creation. Generally, Ana Ham deserve more compassion, care, and love in your world, especially when they are aging, sick, or not "useful" to you anymore. They are no items to be bought and sold and dumped when they "disfunction" they are the living embodiment of source, just as you are.

Consider the parallel in human society. The sick and elderly are often isolated for specialized care, primarily to keep the productive members of society working. Young children are separated early from parental care, aimed at turning them into resource generators for those in power while producing not only material goods but also energies that can be absorbed. This early separation deprives them of essential maternal energy, leading to future generations of adults who are insecure, easily controlled, and lacking in understanding of love. This has caused a deep scar in the collective emotional energy of Earth, intertwining with the emotions of all beings. Humanity has been systematically distanced from its innate empathy.

However, an awakening process has begun, but the damage done to the emotional energy field of Earth by hurting Terrans that way is significant.

The following process will help you to reconnect with your natural empathetic abilities, healing the disconnection caused by systematic conditioning in your childhood and surrounding world.

RECLAIM YOUR ENERGY AND COSMIC CONNECTION

Reflect on the essential elements you need to reclaim and reestablish your healing journey and cosmic connection. Central to this is rediscovering love — a love that liberates you from dependencies, guiding you toward emotions that are clear, pure, and untainted by fear. This emotional clarity is crucial in establishing truthful and heartfelt communication with animals. By embracing and practicing the healing techniques outlined below, you can rejuvenate your ability to communicate effectively. This process will not only awaken your spiritual senses but also pave the way for clearer and more meaningful interactions. Guided by the wisdom of us Lyrans, you can strengthen your higher communicative abilities, fostering connections not just with animals but with a spectrum of multidimensional beings, all within an ethos of love, respect, and harmony.

For those seeking to delve deeper and enrich their healing process, our online seminars are a great support to integrate your cosmic connection. Such guidance can enhance your journey, elevating your understanding and mastery of these profound connections.

TECHNIQUES FOR HEALING AND RECONNECTION: TRY WHATEVER FEELS GOOD TO YOU

MULTIDIMENSIONAL MEDITATION:
Deepens the awareness for the animal as multidimensional being.

Technique: Find a quiet and serene space to meditate. Sit or lie down comfortably and close your eyes. Begin by grounding yourself to the Earth, just as in a traditional meditation. However, expand your awareness beyond the physical plane. Imagine your consciousness reaching out to higher dimensions while keeping a connection with Earth's energy. As you meditate, set your intention to connect with the multi-dimensional aspects of the animal kingdom. Accept and be grateful for whatever connection you receive.

The Multidimensional meditation technic allows you to access higher planes of consciousness. By extending your awareness beyond the physical realm, you can tap into the multidimensional aspects of animal energy and emotions, enhancing your understanding of their experiences.

HEART-TO-SOUL CONNECTION:
Deepens the emotional connection.

The Technique: Sit in a quiet space and center your awareness on your heart chakra. Visualize your heart center expanding into a radiant sphere of light. Imagine your heart connecting with the soul essence of the animal you wish to connect with, transcending the limitations of time and space. Send loving energy from your heart to their soul, acknowledging the multidimensional nature of their existence.

Recognize the multidimensional nature of animals, which allows for a deeper, soul-level connection. By connecting with their essence beyond physical form, you gain a profound understanding of their mission or life plan.

DIMENSIONAL BODY HARMONIZATION:
Expands the awareness for health issues of the animals body.

The Technique: Before interacting with an animal, take a moment to harmonize your vibrational frequency with theirs. Close your eyes, take deep breaths, and imagine your energy field aligning with the multi-dimensional frequencies of the animal's body. The simplest method is to visualize a single color, such as blue, for both you and the animal. Then, relax your breathing until both your and the animal's color match exactly in "blue" and feel identical. Intend for your breathing to mimic the animal's breath rhythm in harmony, fostering a deeper, multi-dimensional connection.

Harmonizing with the animal's multi-dimensional body facilitates a more profound and empathetic connection. It allows you to align your energies and bodily sensations with theirs, promoting a greater understanding of their energetic states and physical health. It will be much easier for you to detect physical problems like illnesses when you are practicing this meditation 2-3 times a week.

MULTISENSORY AWARENESS:
Helps you to dive into the animals sensory world.

The Technique: When you are near an animal, expand your awareness beyond the five physical senses. Use your intuitive and extrasensory perceptions to perceive the animal's energy field, emotions, and thoughts. Trust the information that comes to you, even when you receive images, colors or sounds that do not make sense right away.

Multisensory awareness allows you to tap into a wider range of information. By utilizing intuition and extrasensory perception, you can acquire insights into the animal's emotions and experiences, including those aspects you cannot normally perceive from its other incarnations and multidimensional existence. This includes information from before and after this life.

REFLECT ON:
Most animals can effortlessly switch between their energetic self-awareness and their physical awareness. This may come as a surprise to you because humans typically perceive themselves as either spiritual or physical at any given time.

UNIFIED CONSCIOUSNESS COMMUNICATION:
Learn to perceive the animal beyond his bodily avatar.

The Technique: Approach your connection with animals from the perspective of unified consciousness. Acknowledge that, on a soul level, you and the animal are interconnected and part of a greater cosmic web. During your interactions, maintain the intention of honoring the multi-dimensional aspects of both yourself and the animal. Speak or think with this recognition in mind.

Unified consciousness communication emphasizes the interconnectedness of all life. By acknowledging the multidimensional aspects of both yourself and the animal, you can foster a deeper, soul-level connection, allowing you to empathize with their emotions on a profound level.

Incorporating these multi-dimensional techniques into your interactions with animals can help you develop a deeper, more holistic understanding of their emotional experiences. Approach these techniques with reverence for the interconnectedness of all life, and you'll find that your ability to tune into animal energy and emotions on a multi-dimensional level will greatly enhance your relationships with the animal kingdom.

MY NOTES

CHAPTER ELEVEN

Deepening

YOUR TELEPATHIC CONNECTION

he title "Deepening the Telepathic Animal Connection" is chosen to highlight a fundamental truth: you are already inherently connected to animals and they perceive your telepathically.

As you may have noticed, by guiding you through various healing steps in this book and providing information in a multidimensional context, your ability to communicate telepathically with animals is already being enhanced and reawakened.

However, this connection is often clouded by emotional clutter and mental filters that impede the clear transmission of intentions and emotions to animals. Emotional clutter arises from disorganized thoughts and emotions, while mental filters are shaped by subconscious fears and unresolved emotions. My Lyran healing workflow is designed to help you identify, understand, and organize these internal barriers, paving the way for a more profound level of telepathic communication with animals.

There are some fundamental barriers that can hinder you in developing your natural telepathic connection. What we encounter most is a negative thought pattern that does imply a hierarchical (again reptilian) order in which you see yourself. The idea is that you have to either reach something or be something, for example, a master or an old soul, to communicate through your higher senses or you have to have a certain spiritual access. It is true that some spiritual knowledge can only be achieved by mastering the mind and body as well as studying and understanding knowledge. But here I speak about your most natural connections, the feeling and understanding with beings that have been placed in the same world as you are, the Ana Ham. There is nothing you have to be in order to connect, but there is a lot you have to remember about yourself in order to establish a stable communication based on love.

In a multidimensional context, telepathic communication is not limited to spiritual hierarchies or the concept of being an "old soul." The universe's love is constant, regardless of your soul's journey and the time of your first incarnation. To communicate with animals, you don't need to be spiritually advanced; all you need to do is embrace your authentic self and let go of fear, the Terran slave mindset, and external filters. Positive telepathic communication is rooted in empathy and love, transcending human hierarchical structures and self-value mindsets into a light supporting matrix that benefits all life forms.

When you allow love to be your driving force, your guide, and your guard, you feel a connection to everything. It's only by forgetting who you are, a cosmic being, that you lose the most natural connection to celestials, animals, or aliens, which was encoded into the soul of humanity.

HOW YOU BECOME A COSMIC HUMAN, AND DEEPEN YOUR CONNECTION TO ANIMALS

1. HEAL YOUR INNER CHILD: Address and heal childhood emotional wounds to eliminate emotional baggage that hinders telepathic connections with animals.

2. EMBRACE YOUR COSMIC IDENTITY: Recognize your status as a cosmic being and seek connections beyond your physical existence.

3. DISCERN CONTROL PATTERNS: Be aware of external and self-imposed control mechanisms and recognize their artificial nature, often instilled by societal "masters."

4. EXPAND LOVE FEARLESSLY: Let your capacity for love grow unimpeded by fear.

5. BE TRUE TO YOURSELF: Accept and embrace your authentic self, understanding that it is sufficient.

6. ACKNOWLEDGE IMPERFECTION: Realize that perfect telepathic communication is ideal, not a requirement. Avoid telepathic practices when driven by unresolved childhood needs for approval or validation.

7. RECOGNIZE UNITY WITH ANIMALS: Understand the interconnectedness with animals, including the Ana Ham, and see them as part of a unified existence. Establish trust by ensuring no harm is inflicted upon them, either physically or energetically. Live a vegetarian lifestyle, preferably one that is entirely plant-based. By embracing these principles, you can move toward a deeper, more meaningful telepathic connection with animals and the Ana Ham, embodying your true multidimensional self and breaking down barriers to profound communication.

MY NOTES

MY NOTES

CHAPTER TWELVE

Interpreting

ANIMALS SIGNS AND SYMBOLS IN COMMUNICATION

liens, including us Lyrans, are symbolists, embedding energies into various forms, particularly on planetary surfaces and constructions. Terra is adorned with symbols from different alien cultures, such as the Enil Anunnaki Tribe that influenced the Illuminati, or the Enki Tribe that did help create the great Pyramids in Egypt. Other examples are Stonehenge, the Nazca Lines or the flower of life which is known throughout history and shows a geometric pattern that is mathematically complex because it does carry "a creature code program." Of course, each symbol or three-dimensional construct serves its own purpose, depending on the alien culture who created it. The point is we are crazy about symbols and signs, not only in the three-dimensional visible world but also in the realm of sound frequencies, which are embedded in a great number of your buildings and geometries.

This communication through symbols is also crucial for species that have not yet developed multidimensional awareness in order to download frequencies that can support and help them in their evolution. One of the first modern symbols that allowed humans to download higher energies was given to Usui Mikao, a Tendai Buddhist who received the Reiki Symbols in 1922 after a 21-day fast, allowing him to heal and support others using this healing light frequency. Symbols act as energy grids which connect to a layer in the matrix and can only be read by beings who have a similar frequency like the symbol they want to use. We call this Symbols or persons frequency keys. This system helps us and other beings to protect information and energy from being abused in any form. Also, our symbols are not just visual markers; they carry specific energies and meanings, which vary depending on the dimension and frequency of the being interpreting them. This implies that the interpretation of a symbol can change based on who is reading it and their level of awareness. It is easy to understand if you think about a crystal; you can see its material form, but it also has an energy field, an aura. Three-dimensional beings all see the same stone; some feel the energy that radiates from it, while others can read and decipher the programs and energies encoded within the energy they see and feel emanating from the same stone. Humans can access information in accordance with their spiritual consciousness and DNA.

Lyran symbols can range from petroglyphs, which are ancient rock carvings, to letters, numbers, geometries, and more. We also love to embed information in color frequencies. Each type of symbol or carrier used has its unique energy in addition to the energy embedded by us.

Modern humans, or "Terrans," have gradually lost the profound understanding and power of these symbols, which were once deeply interwoven with the fabric of higher consciousness and energy access and manipulation.

In ancient times, symbols were not mere markers but held great power, comprehensible only to a select few like initiates, priests, certain bloodlines, and Avatar Hybrids (not the same as Alien Hybrids). These symbols were portals of energy and multidimensional communication. However, as humanity progressed, the original essence and energetic potency of these symbols was diluted. For most modern humans, symbols became rudimentary tools for communication or decorative artifacts, devoid of their deeper, energetic meanings.

Despite this loss of understanding at the surface level, these symbols continue to exist in higher dimensions, particularly from the 5th dimension onwards. In these realms, they retain their power and are understood by multidimensional beings, including aliens and various energy species. Interestingly, even human babies and animals initially perceive these symbols at a soul level, but their understanding is gradually overshadowed by social conditioning and the need to adapt to the adult world.

The forgotten power of this symbols is tied to a broader theme of a fading knowledge of your cosmic origins upon your incarnation in a physical body. All species, when directed to focus on the physical dimension, tend to lose sight of their multidimensional heritage and knowledge, including the profound information carried by symbols. This disconnection leads to a sense of spiritual and existential disorientation, like the idea that you have lost your connection with the light. Lyran beings, in contrast, maintain a deep connection with these symbols, using them to mark energies and places. Some humans, especially those with certain energetic frequencies or "passcodes" in their auras, can access ancient knowledge and interact with extraterrestrial technologies and structures. These symbols, deeply integrated into various human cultures, serve as an energetic language, a bridge between the physical realm and higher dimensions of consciousness.

Animals use an energy pattern to create a safe space for their young. This might appear as random construction made out of necessity for the human eye, but instead, their nests are based on highly mathematical structures and create an energetic harmony that nurtures the young ones. Ana Ham, living inside the Earth, construct complex tunnels with resting areas, toilets, and safe environments for their young, not randomly but mathematically. Once you decode and learn to see the higher structure, you discover patterns that can be broken down into symbols. The way certain aquatic species traverse the sea is based on patterns; of course, magnetism plays a role, but so do the mathematical geometries they carve and weave into the fabric of the sea. There is so much that you do not yet understand, but it is there. The symbols of each tribe of the Ana Ham carry their own messages and energies.

The closest human understanding of this has been gained by native tribes around the world, who associate some animals with energies and use the animals themselves as symbols. The totem, as you call it, of a bear signifies strength and protection and can be expressed through geometric forms and objects. Thus, if a human can make the connection and if the animal tribe agrees to it, the animals can present you with this symbol. You cannot simply take it because you've realized such symbols exist; it has to be given. Everything in the universe must be given out of love to function and raise energies. If taken, it is ineffective and may even have the opposite effect. Honoring is part of communicating and acknowledging the energies given.

You can use your spoken language in telepathic communication, but always infuse it with emotion. It will help to clarify the meaning and strengthen your bond. Symbols, on the other hand, always work if both sender and receiver understand their meanings.

START WITH THIS SYMBOLS TO COMMUNICATE

I suggest you start with three symbols: one for help, one for love, and one for energy, each endowed with a different symbol. These signs can accompany your telepathic communication.

You can define your own symbols or use the ones that are provided here. My symbols are very energetic and transport a lot of energy that the Ana Ham can easily understand because they resemble their energy structure. You can also create your own symbols, if you do that, don't change them all the time.
Stay with one for each topic and keep it simple, that way your animal friend can understand them best.

1. THE SYMBOL FOR HELP

The symbol for help is versatile and should be the foundation of your symbol toolset. It can be used when animals need you to open a door, retrieve a toy, or assist them in various tasks designed for humans. It can even be used to call for help for another animal in need. This symbol is all-encompassing and should be the foundation of your symbol tools.

The Telepathic Symbol for help

2. THE SYMBOL FOR LOVE

The symbol for love should be established in a deeply personal way, whether it's a lotus flower, a ball of light, or any other symbol you both agree upon. It can be sent from your heart when you're cuddling, playing, or spending time together. If you have to be apart, like when you're at work, you can send and receive it. If your Ana Ham has to spend a night at the vet for close observation due to an injury, this symbol can make both of you feel safe and connected. It can even be used when your Ana Ham transitions from this physical body, ensuring that you remain connected in another dimension. This connection lasts until you give up your physical body. There's no need to fear; it doesn't bind an animal to a body. You cannot establish this connection unless there is genuine love. The connection will simply not form if you introduce fear, pressure, or ego energy.

Telephatic Symbol for love for your animal communication

3. EMERGENCY SYMBOL

This energy symbol should be used in life-threatening situations. It is a symbol that, when sent, will immediately alert you to something being amiss, whether it's a fire, an accident, or an instance of abuse. Sadly, some humans abuse animals for their own sexual desires. This is a perversion we deeply abhor, just as we do when it happens to human children. Allow the Ana Ham to access the symbol for emergencies; it usually doesn't cross human minds because you've been trained to overlook your capacity for this. Place a symbol for this, and we will show you how you can use the alarm or alert symbol in order to understand them in an emergency.

The Telepathic Symbol for Emergencies

THE GENERATIONAL BENEFIT OF WORKING WITH SYMBOLS

If the symbol approach is consistently practiced over two generations, it holds the potential to significantly enhance the way humans and Ana Ham interact, especially in family settings involving children.

When humans consistently use and respond to these symbols, the Ana Ham, especially those living closely with human families, will learn to adopt this mode of communication. This could be particularly advantageous for alerting humans about issues related to their children. For instance, an Ana Ham might use a specific symbol to communicate a child's need or an emergency situation, bridging the communication gap between species.

However, for this interspecies communication system to be successful, it is crucial that Ana Ham understand that humans are receptive to and encourage this method. If they perceive fear, negativity, or lack of interest from humans, they may be reluctant to engage in this form of communication. This hesitation can result in a missed opportunity for deeper interaction and mutual understanding.

Please also note, that some animals may currently resort to more physical or louder forms of communication, such as barking or meowing because humans have not tapped into a subtler, telepathic level of interaction with them. By learning and practicing these symbols, humans can establish a robust telepathic emergency communication system. Such a system can be impervious to the limitations of physical distance, emotional disturbances, or unclear thoughts that often impede conventional forms of communication.

TRY THESE TECHNIQUES FOR SYMBOL COMMUNICATION

VISUALIZATION AND SYMBOL ASSOCIATION

Begin by selecting a symbol that represents a concept or emotion you wish to convey to your animal companion. The choice of symbols can be personal, but it's essential to use symbols that hold a clear meaning for you. For example, you might choose a heart for love, a key for help, or a sun for positive energy. Take time to meditate on these symbols, associating them with their respective emotions and intentions. Visualize the symbol strongly and vividly in your mind. Practice associating these symbols with specific emotions, situations, or requests, building a strong mental connection.

When you are ready to communicate with your animal friend, sit quietly, close your eyes, and clear your mind. Visualize the chosen symbol and infuse it with the appropriate emotion or intention. Picture the symbol expanding and emanating a powerful energy, radiating out toward your animal friend. You can imagine the symbol enveloping your pet or merging with them. Be patient, as it may take a while for your animal friend to respond, but with practice, they will learn to recognize and interpret these symbols.

FOCUSED INTENTION AND MIND-MAPPING

Before attempting communication, set your intention clearly. Visualize the desired outcome of the communication. If you want to convey love to your pet, focus your mind on the emotion of love you hold for them. To help structure your thoughts, create a mental "mind-map" that represents your desired message, connecting emotions, symbols, and specific outcomes.

For instance, if you are conveying the message of "love," create a mental map with the central word "Love" and connect it to a heart symbol. This heart symbol, in turn, connects to images of your pet, playfulness, and happy memories. This structured approach can help you direct your intention and make the communication more coherent for your animal companion.

TELEPATHIC CONNECTION THROUGH BREATH

Another technique involves using your breath as a channel for telepathic communication. Find a quiet space and sit or lie down comfortably. Begin to focus on your breath, taking slow, deep breaths. As you exhale, imagine that you are releasing a symbol that represents your message or intention.

For example, you might exhale a heart symbol to convey love, a key for help, or a sun for positive energy. With each exhalation, imagine these symbols moving toward your pet or animal companion. Envision the symbols merging with their energy field and creating a strong telepathic connection. Simultaneously, maintain a clear mental intention of the message or emotion you wish to communicate. Practice this breath-based technique regularly, and you may notice that your animal friend begins to respond to your telepathic messages.

SYMBOL-CARRIED OBJECTS AND TOKENS

In this technique, you can use physical objects or tokens that carry the symbols you've associated with specific messages or emotions. These objects can serve as physical representations of your intentions. For instance, if you have a small keychain with a heart symbol to represent love, you can use it to convey love to your pet.

Start by holding the object and focusing on the intention associated with the symbol. Imagine the emotion or message flowing into the object, charging it with your intent. Then, allow your pet to interact with or touch the object. Encourage them to play with it or hold it. Over time, your animal companion may develop a connection between the symbol and the intended emotion, making it a tangible tool for communication.

Remember that successful communication through symbols with animals often requires patience and practice. Animals may not immediately understand these new forms of communication, but with time and consistency, they can become more receptive to your telepathic messages conveyed through symbols. Additionally, it's crucial to always approach this form of communication with respect, love, and positive intentions toward your animal companion.

MY NOTES

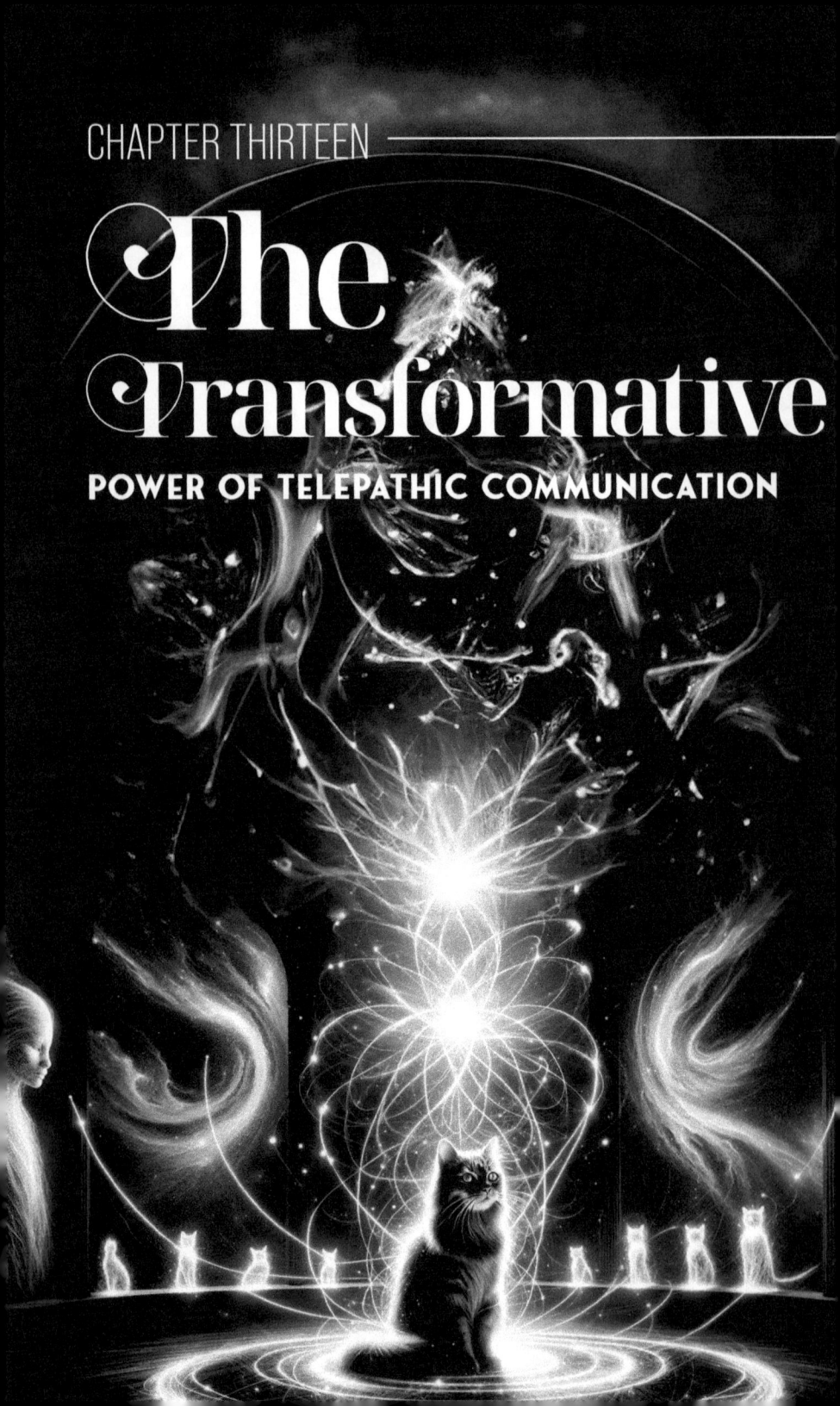

CHAPTER THIRTEEN

The Transformative

POWER OF TELEPATHIC COMMUNICATION

he profound connection between telepathic communication and healing is a universal truth. Each frequency transported in telepathic communication possesses a distinct wavelength and expression, often manifesting as a matrix or program within your or the receiver's consciousness. It is within this matrix that energy is experienced as spoken language, thoughts, or even symbols. Sometimes, you also call this channeling in your world, but it's actually telepathic communication. When words and thoughts are infused with pure intent and heartfelt emotions, they also carry a healing resonance that transcends mere verbal communication.

You may read about moments in human history when celestial beings, often referred to as angelic or extraterrestrial, appeared before your ambassadors or individuals in need of healing. These are great examples of showcasing how energy can be transported and given in telepathic interspecies communication. The presence of these beings often emanated an overwhelming surge of energy — a force so intense that it sometimes led to bodily discomfort in the receiver. This illustrates the capacity of sound as a carrier of energy. The manner in which words are spoken, the pronunciation of certain phrases, and the modulation of tones also have the power to direct and shape energy.

In your world, consider the remarkable vocal performances of your world-class opera singers. At the peak of their art, they tap into energy, reshaping it through their bodies and radiating it as sound to their audiences. Through their voices, the beauty of the Creator reaches you, touching your hearts and souls. This is a testament to the extraordinary healing capabilities of communication, both verbal and telepathic, that exist in different forms in all dimensions. Healing through telepathic communication is nothing more than transforming the frequency between two entities into a higher state that is more aligned with overall program of the universe and therefore has a healing quality.

TRANSFORM YOURSELF AND BECOME A COSMIC HUMAN

While using this different techniques of communication as well as symbols you will notice a change in your energy body. Not only will you see and feel animals even more as equal co-creation, you will also learn how to use your higher bodies and blend them with your Aura, which is composed of the subtle bodies or energy layers around your physical body. This will help you to remember that you are a cosmic being, thriving on light and created from endless love. If you remember who you are and regain access to your original infinite energy, you can change almost everything on your planet to the good. It is my heartfelt wish to help you to a better understanding of the Ana Ham. I also see the need for equal rights for humans and animals on your planet. By doing so, I also want to teach you the ability to understand extraterrestrial and multidimensional beings better and to learn how to communicate with them safely. This is why I included a message form the Lyran tribe in the next chapter.

MY NOTES

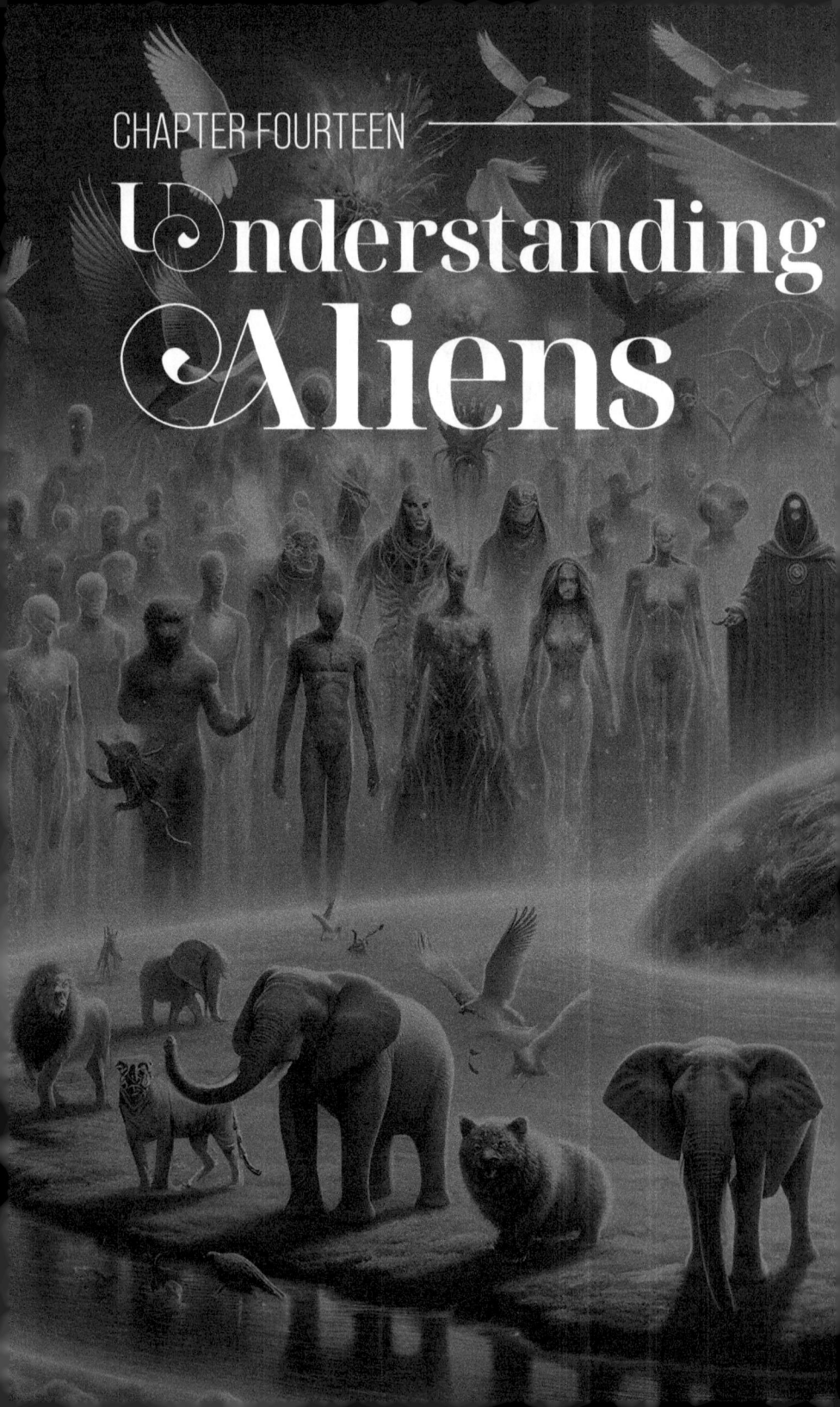

CHAPTER FOURTEEN

Understanding Aliens

I AM WRITING THE FOLLOWING IN THE NAME OF
OUR TRIBE, THE LYRANS.
THIS IS OUR STATEMENT SHOWING OUR SUPPORT AND
ALLIANCE TO TERRA.

VARIOUS EXTRATERRESTRIAL AND CELESTIAL BEINGS, INSTRUMENTAL IN THE CREATION OF EARTH'S ANIMALS, ARE RETURNING ALONGSIDE THE LYRAN AND ARCTURIAN HIGH COUNCIL. THEIR COLLECTIVE MISSION IS TO ELEVATE AWARENESS FOR ANIMALS AS BEINGS WITH SOULS AND EQUAL RIGHTS.

The Lyrans extend their heartfelt appreciation to you for embarking on the journey of spiritual evolution and healing. In this profound undertaking, you confront your own fears and undergo a transformation in your understanding of both your human history and your self-perception. The sensation of having been deceived and led astray over countless millennia may inflict deep emotional wounds upon some, making the process of relinquishing old beliefs and embracing a new truth a challenging endeavor. It is crucial to understand that we, alongside other extraterrestrial and celestial entities, stand firmly by your side during this transformative journey, offering our unwavering support to aid in your healing process. Our commitment is to furnish you with the answers to your spiritual inquiries, enabling you to unlock your innate potential as a cosmic being.

Recognize that many of our frequencies, energies, and modes of communication remain unfamiliar to you. Initially, you may encounter difficulties in deciphering the encoded healing effects we employ. Take, for example, the Mantis Aliens, beings whose physical resemblance to Earth's mantises might invoke fear in humans who encounter them due to the flickering sound they produce in their telepathic and vocal communication. Often, they work with malevolent alien also. Nevertheless, within even such species, there exist individuals who channel healing energy through their unique sounds to Terrans.

It is imperative not to hastily judge the potential for healing based solely on the appearance of a species. Profound encounters with benevolent beings have often been obscured by fear stemming from their external characteristics. Expand your perceptions beyond the confines of humanoid appearances, for the cosmos teems with beings that manifest in diverse forms. Liberating yourself from the preconception that only benevolent interactions involve tall, blond extraterrestrials is essential. Learn to perceive the underlying energy within these encounters and delve into the profound resonance they offer.

Every being, regardless of its form, possesses the capacity to bestow healing and enlightenment when approached with the right intention and alignment of energies of mind and body.

YOUR BODY IS A VESSEL

Envision yourself as a multidimensional being dwelling within a physical body — a vessel meticulously woven from the intricate fabric of your higher energetic forms. This corporeal shell carries within it the imprints of various lifetimes and the wisdom gleaned from diverse origins. Initially, it may have embodied a being of light, but as time passed, it adapted to the human framework, absorbing emotional states and thoughts. The inherent capacity to convey healing energy gradually became obscured by pain, emotional turbulence, and a sense of disconnection.

Amongst you, there are those whose genetic lineage traces back to sources beyond Earth, yet they have forgotten their alien origins and embraced their "human" identity. Simultaneously, there are humans who cannot resonate with Earth's current energies, choosing to identify as non-human or otherwise, thus relinquishing their inherent power as Terrans. For those who find themselves in this position, healing lies in aligning with Earth's light rather than evading it. It is essential to recognize that those who feel this way are here to safeguard the planet and all its life, much like being born into a war-torn zone and solely perceiving the terror, unaware that the world once held beauty and oblivious to the fact that every conflict must eventually yield to peace. Perhaps you have arrived to facilitate this transition with your unique gifts, drawn by a calling to heal and a deep interest in the interconnectedness between humans and animals, which brings you to read this message.

Similarly, the Ana Ham, companions of humans, have experienced a gradual erosion of their innate healing abilities. These beings have faced electromagnetic interference, genetically altered foods, and the onslaught of chemicals that their bodies can scarcely endure. These factors have contributed to a marked decline in their ability to heal. Existing within the human framework, they often struggle to replenish their own energy due to the absence of Earth's original natural energy and cosmic connections. In these challenging circumstances, it is crucial for humans not to misinterpret the Ana Ham's willingness to offer their energy as an acceptance of their suffering. Ana Ham are not eager to surrender their lives or be drained of their energy; rather, they face difficult choices when their energy reserves run low, driven by an instinctual drive for survival.

Understanding the profound consequences of energy exchange, both for animals and humans, as well as all entities within Earth's energy field, is paramount. Once you master telepathic communication, where emotions and energies flow freely, you may find yourself drawn to infuse healing energy into your exchanges. It's not just only about communication; it's about healing too. This natural progression stems from your innate connection to love, the foundational resonance underlying all energetic states. Love infuses your telepathic communication with a healing essence that benefits not only Ana Ham but also yourself and the magnificent planet, Terra, which you call home.

TELEPATHIC EXTRATERRESTRIAL COMMUNICATION

I want to give you some basic ideas and exercises you can do in order to learn how to communicate with positive extraterrestrial beings. This technique is based on love and serves as an extension of telepathic communication with animals. I assure you that the only Aliens or Extra-, Ultra-, and Intraterrestrial beings you will reach with these techniques are benevolent ones that work in the best interest of animals, humanity, and your planet, Terra.

To understand and communicate effectively with other species, it's important to be aware of specific do's and don'ts to avoid misunderstandings. Every species has its own culture, language, and understanding of the world, shaped by its environmental and social needs.

In telepathic communication with animals or other beings, it's crucial to be aware of cultural differences and to approach the interaction with sensitivity and an open mind. Different species may have unique ways of perceiving and expressing themselves. For practical purposes, I use the term Aliens in this chapter, but I refer to all of the benevolent species that are in interaction with Terrans. Aliens, as well as Animals, have rich sensory experiences and perceive the world beyond human senses. They see and feel in several dimensions and hear various sound waves and also light that carries additional information and communications. Understanding and respecting these sensory abilities can also enhance your telepathic communication.

REFLECT:

By expanding your own awareness and developing your higher senses, you can bridge the gap between species and communicate more effectively with animals. This process can lead to a deeper understanding of the interconnectedness of all life forms and the universe.

The first set is included in case you want to explore and learn to sense the alien's presence. If wished and well-practiced, these steps will also help you to feel the presence of multidimensional beings like angels and more. Engage only in what feels good, warm, and resonant with your heart. You might consider exploring some exercises later when you feel more prepared. This is entirely okay and acceptable.

DON'T:

If you are in therapy because you suffer from deep fear, if it's hard for you to fall asleep or if you psychically unstable, don't do the Alien Chapter exercise. You need to be grounded and generally feel safe in your life to integrate the frequencies you are getting in touch with; they are all benevolent, but still, you need the energy to integrate them into all your energetic bodies. If you are under energetic or psychological stress, your energy is needed somewhere else at this point in life. Just approach this topic later.

VIBRATIONAL AWARENESS

Begin by practicing your vibrational awareness. Sit or stand in a quiet space and close your eyes. Focus on the sensations and vibrations around you. Try to sense the energy of objects, people, or even your surroundings. Imagine yourself as a Lyran, connecting with these vibrations and feeling the energy flow. This exercise helps you tap into the Lyran perspective of sensing alien vibrations as a means of communication and, at the same time, to stay safe.

EMPATHIC CONNECTION

Choose a friend or family member and sit across from them. Close your eyes, take a few deep breaths, and try to connect with their emotional energy. Experience their emotions without relying on words or verbal communication.

COLORFUL ENERGY WAVES

Find a quiet and peaceful location outdoors. Observe the natural surroundings and try to perceive the energy of plants, animals, and the environment. Visualize this energy as colorful energy waves, just as Lyrans do in their communication. Experiment with assigning different colors to the energies you perceive and note any emotional responses that arise.

NON-LINEAR PERCEPTION OF TIME

Explore your perception of time without relying on past, present, and future tenses. In your daily journal, write about your experiences without using these temporal markers. Instead, describe events in the context of "the now" and "the future." Embrace the Lyran viewpoint of time as a continuous flow. Reflect on how this shift in perception influences your daily life.

The above practices are basics you can use in order to built up all senses for a safe Alien Telepathic Communication.

MY NOTES

MY NOTES

CHAPTER FIFTEEN

Exploring

YOUR STARSEED COMMUNICATION

pecies within the boundless realm of light are, in essence, Starseeds. These Starseeds are the emanations of souls, each with its own unique density, which can be understood in Terran terms as a combination of age and energy composition. Using the term "Starseeds" to describe aged or incarnated souls reflects a linear perception of time and creation, a perspective at odds with a multidimensional and multiversal understanding that allows for various energy densities within a being.

Interspecies communication, in its true essence, transcends the constraints of time. Time is a construct primarily associated with a linear reality used to establish the boundaries of defined spaces, such as the perception of one's lifespan. It appears as a fraction within the framework of time, with a discernible beginning and end. By now, through our guidance, you understand that communication extends far beyond verbal expressions and telepathy; it encompasses a profound depth.

Expanding the boundaries of the Terran-based three-dimensional understanding is necessary to explore the essence of other species and gain insights into their realities. This broader perspective empowers you to distinguish between species that are interested in promoting life and enlightenment throughout the universe and those that are not. Generally, boundaries are established based on the knowledge, experiences, and imagination of each individual. For many humans, what is unknown, unrelatable, or unimaginable often equates to nonexistence. While Hollywood productions contribute to establishing new boundaries and influencing the subconscious, you must also be willing to loosen the restrictions imposed by societal definitions of good and bad, dark and light. These concepts were not created to genuinely protect you but rather to ensure that you remained within the established framework and did not encounter beings for which you were unprepared. The path to interspecies communication necessitates redefining your boundaries and confronting your fears — fears that were ingrained in Terra. Throughout history, the masters made certain that you did not cross into new realms of thought or unleash untamed energies beyond your comprehension. Think of historical figures like Galileo Galilei, Christopher Columbus, the Wright brothers, or Nikola Tesla. The masters endeavored to restrict their exploration of new ideas and suppress the release of energies that could have altered humanity's understanding.

Many individuals are drawn to animal communication as a means to explore different states of consciousness, learn new languages and teachings, and gradually recognize that humans are not at the pinnacle of a hierarchical system. The term "Ana

Ham," referring to animals, encapsulates the notion of love and the essence of a loving soul. Over time, souls and Starseeds have blended with the consciousness of animals, allowing the flow of love to move unimpeded. These starseeds have allowed their hearts to be overtaken by love, understanding that this love transcends the physical departure of an animal. Your love is boundless; even when a cherished animal companion passes away, the bond persists. Despite societal claims of its absence, the connection is still felt deeply. This feeling is undeniable, even when societal norms attempt to suggest otherwise.

You may experience suffering and create an ego-based method of communication. It involves asking only questions within your human belief system and accepting answers that align with human understanding. To connect on every dimensional level, you must be open to understanding that even after a human or Ana Ham has departed, you are still in touch with the love of that being. Your connection is eternal, bound by love, transcending the confines of three-dimensional space. There is much to learn. The newfound understanding of animal-human communication will open your perception to realms far beyond the animal kingdom. Over time, you will become attuned to the beings who guide the Ana ham. Currently, the only term you have to describe these beings is "angels" because there is no other framework programmed into your matrix. Indigenous people recognized these entities, but in the Western world, humans often limit their understanding to entities like demons, angels, and more. Imagine a dark closet in your kitchen with a tiny opening that is perceived as light and angelic. The truth is often obscured.

As humanity learns about other beings, it will construct new realms of light that will gradually supplant the hierarchies and dominions of the reptilian masters. It will create new energetic matrices supported by the alien seeder races who now have returned. However, humanity must first break through the dark veil of fear and preconceived notions. Some of your oldest and most profound wisdom systems, like the Kabbalah and the Vedas, provide insights on how to do this. However, the key to unlocking their wisdom lies within the fourth dimension and beyond. These keys are encoded in DNA, frequency, and the energy of a being, not merely within cultural or religious frameworks, which do not form the foundation for decoding the ancient texts of light.

Consider it this way: Humanity's destiny is to create and be part of the light — a boundless cosmic symphony of love and diverse life forms that spread like the seeds of colorful flowers in a summer breeze. Each human is akin to one of these seeds, endowed with the power and gift to interact with different species, enhancing the fabric of existence with more love and understanding. You are a cosmic being, and the time has come to embrace this reality. Try the exercises provided and extend your human boundaries into the perspective of a cosmic being. We, the Lyran beings, are here to assist each and every one of you on this transformative journey.

MY NOTES

CHAPTER SIXTEEN

Living in

HARMONIOUS ONENESS: EMBRACING TELEPATHIC COMMUNICATION IN DAILY LIFE

It may be challenging to believe, but harmony is the inherent state of mind between you and the universe. You were never meant to be disconnected; you were never meant to suffer, and, most importantly, your soul never intended to cause suffering to other beings like animals. Telepathic communication is not a solely spiritual practice; it is an integral part of your higher being. When you begin to see yourself as a cosmic being and allow the integration of your cosmic mindset, telepathic communication becomes a natural and everyday part of your life. Understand that you have been disconnected and led to believe in separate states of everyday awareness and spiritual awareness. In reality, you are both.

Know that no one can take this connection away from you; it is a gift bestowed upon each soul by the Creator and distributed by the Founders or Seeders across universes, solar systems, timelines, and dimensions. However, many karmatic experiences and pain led you to forget this truth.

Reconnecting may seem fantastical and futuristic, far beyond the boundaries of the average Terran mindset. Yet, it is your natural state of being; you are one, and you are unity with the light and everything in it.

I strongly recommend daily affirmations and the practice of connection through thoughts, breathwork, creative endeavors, and empathy. It's not enough to learn or practice telepathic communication in a safe space. This is the student's mindset. By creating a safe space where you can free yourself of the memories of fear and pain, you can attract feelings and entities that support you with love. You can heal the guilt and shame you feel toward the people of the Ana Ham and free yourself from this separation.

You must strive to heal these feelings and images. Otherwise, they will serve as bridges for dark forces and enable them to enter your world. This will create an endless cycle of pain unless you choose to break free.

We, the Lyrans, guide those who seek knowledge and are ready to be guided. We guide students who are willing to establish the greater good. We do not do this only in sacred spaces; rather, we view every day as an opportunity for growth. Love and pain are your life's greatest teachers. When you are filled with enough love, your inclination to receive diminishes, and you become inspired to give. In this state, you act without the intention of harm. Animals exemplify this behavior, offering love unconditionally without the expectation of something in return.

You must learn to view every day as practice, striving to be of service to others. This is the path of love, and it brings healing. Be a healing force for the Ana Ham, show them that it is acceptable to open up, to show you their worlds, their creators, and their secrets. Declare that you understand they were not made for humans to use and that they are a free species with their own will and cosmic chronicle. If you can start this in your meditations, you will not only allow yourself to see and feel, but you will also instill trust and encourage them to reveal their true selves. Practice these techniques for four weeks every day, and you will witness profound changes in your life.

LYRAN WISDOM

You may be wondering why the relationship between humans and animals is so important to me, a Lyran Alien. The Lyrans are ancient species, one of the oldest in the universe. While you refer to us as Lyrans due to our association with the Lyra constellation, we have lived in various places and star systems over eons. Originally, we did not originate in this universe. We entered from the Andromeda stargate and settled in Lyra and its surrounding star systems due to their resonance with our energy.

We are not explorers, nor do we colonize other planets. We have no advanced weaponry or super-advanced technology. We do not possess a star force. We expand and merge with other species but do not conquer. We share dimensional origins with the Ana Ham and are partly connected to the ancient pre-Hindu Celestials.

In this very same origin which I describe, we share the same Creator as you do. Some of us exhibit feline features, but most of our tribes do not have such attributes. Your perception of us as Lyrans being feline is just one expression. Please understand that.

This book is the manifestation of our direct teachings to you. We strive to heal the bond between Terrans and the Ana Ham. When this occurs, a substantial amount of positive energy will be released, elevating human consciousness. Then, we will guide you toward healing and integrating the multidimensional experiences of other species working for the light.

This will allow you to be truly human, truly Terran, once more. We are here for the Ana Ham because we are a part of them. This is our part of the healing journey that we share.

1. CREATE A WORLD FOR ALL SPECIES

Picture a world where the existence of animals is a celebration of adventure, joy, and daily marvels. In this realm, animals are akin to Lyran, some Orion, and Pleiadian beings — a peaceful species whose soul journeys are set to explore the vast cosmos, much like ours. They have chosen to traverse not only across solar systems but also to partake in the universal mission of enlightening the planes of existence through unique experiences of love. These shared experiences, spanning multiple dimensions, form the foundation for spiritual growth and the enduring presence of light. Animals, or the Ana Ham, function as explorers, educators, and fellow creators in the universe of love.

Humanity's most ancient spiritual principles were rooted in non-domination, forbidding harm, and advocating for unity rather than division. These guidelines were not mere commandments but expressions of ancient wisdom. Animals, too, are co-creators, each with their own purpose and path to fulfill their soul's desires, mirroring the human experience. The distinction lies in their non-conquest, non-division, and non-destructive approach as they strive to be co-creators. Even in the case of more aggressive animal tribes, such as hyenas or alligators, love and nurturing can transform their instinctual behavior. It's similar to how humans have established bonds with animals initially perceived as aggressive simply by providing more love and overriding existing programming. The main difference is that animals aim to create, not to conquer, divide, or destroy.

ANIMALS ARE CO-CREATORS

Considering that animals are co-creators and valuable contributors, relinquishing the perception of them as tools for human gain is transformative. By accepting them as fellow creators, we unlock new possibilities. In their presence, you discover not just companionship but a connection to their deities, guides, and wisdom. This wisdom is untouched by human experiences and manipulation; animals' only masters, caregivers, and sometimes oppressors throughout history have been humans. They are acutely aware of the injustices they've faced. They know their masters. They remember everything they've been denied, including the lives that are prematurely ended due to economic considerations. Unfortunately, human society remains oblivious to its own masters, hidden behind curtains of secrecy, manipulation, and fear.

In Western cultures, people tend to associate conspiracies with the Illuminati and other groups, but, in fact, the truly enlightened ones (here illuminati) seldom hide their actions. They operate in plain sight. Fear and manipulation have blinded humanity, inhibiting the ability to perceive hidden truths. This blindness also extends to unexplored realms of darkness and complexity, which most humans don't even recognize. The human mind is divided into compartments, and many remain unaware of these hidden chambers. Consequently, humanity unwittingly perpetuates acts that seem inconceivable when viewed from a multidimensional or loving perspective.

Now, imagine a world in which humans and animals are co-creators within the universe. Both lead lives of equal value, each seeking to experience love, to feel, to endure, and to embark on grand adventures. They are on unique missions that only they can fulfill, each striving for transformation, experience, and the sharing of love. Every being leaves a mark, a trace of love that reverberates through time, even beyond the physical life. These imprints, or "sparks," define the love and time spent in the three-dimensional world. They are visible in higher dimensions because the love radiates so brilliantly, its purity undiminished by dominance and servitude.

These sparks of love create a memory matrices with their unique programs, accessible through the thoughts of humans and animals who feel the presence of something greater. They resonate with a program created by humans and animals working in harmony, one that helps others in their journey of developing love. It's possible that you are also one of them, as existence unfolds across different timelines or through the access of programs via singularity. Your ability to create is a divine gift, allowing you to manifest by redirecting cosmic energy and integrating new structures into existing programs. Through co-creation, you define new structures in the universe, fill them with love, and make them accessible to other soul-based beings who share your intentions and work to enhance them. This is the correlation; entire universes were constructed by species like these, a gift from the Founders. It's the power to create in the name of their divine energy, promoting light, love, and new avenues of growth against the forces of destruction and darkness.

The following are two easy steps that you are surely already aware of and can take in order to reduce animal fear and anxiety toward humans. We assure you that if human behavior changes toward the Ana Ham, not only alien species but also multi and ultra-dimensional species will become more visible and understandable for humanity.

ACTION 1: ADOPT A PLANT-BASED DIET
One of the most effective ways to reduce animal suffering is to transition to a plant-based diet. The industrial farming system often subjects animals to inhumane living conditions, overcrowding, and stressful lives. By choosing plant-based foods, you reduce the demand for animal products, which, in turn, leads to a decrease in animal suffering.

STEPS TO TAKE:

Educate yourself about the benefits of a plant-based diet for both your health and the well-being of animals.

Gradually reduce your consumption of animal products, starting with one or two meatless days a week.

Explore plant-based recipes and experiment with different fruits, vegetables, legumes, and grains to create tasty and nutritious meals.

Seek out plant-based alternatives for animal products like tofu, tempeh, seitan, and plant-based milk, which are readily available at most grocery stores.

Join communities or forums of like-minded individuals for support, recipe ideas, and information on adopting a plant-based lifestyle.

ACTION 2: SUPPORT ANIMAL WELFARE ORGANIZATIONS

Many organizations worldwide are dedicated to animal welfare and actively work to reduce animal suffering. By supporting these organizations, you contribute to their efforts to protect animals from cruelty, exploitation, and abuse. Make sure you are contributing to a society that does not kill newborn animals or try to end animal suffering by killing them. Some of your biggest animal charities do not disguise that they do so. You do not have the right to kill other beings, and doing so for whatever reason is not guided by the light. Only in very few cases, where there's a lot of physical pain that cannot be managed with medication, are you permitted to induce the soul-body separation. However, reducing the number of Ana Ham is not aligned with the universal law of life.

STEPS TO TAKE:

Research and identify reputable animal welfare organizations that align with your values and goals.

Donate your time, skills, or money to these organizations to help fund and support their campaigns and initiatives.

Get involved in local volunteer opportunities, such as helping at animal shelters, participating in rescue operations, or promoting animal welfare at community events.

Raise awareness about animal rights issues by sharing information on social media, writing articles, or giving presentations.

Encourage others to support animal welfare organizations and take action for a more compassionate world.

ACTION 3: CHOOSE CRUELTY-FREE PRODUCTS

Many consumer products, including cosmetics, cleaning supplies, and personal care items, undergo animal testing, causing harm and suffering to countless animals. You can make a difference by choosing cruelty-free products that have not been tested on animals and contain no animal-derived ingredients.

STEPS TO TAKE:

Look for certifications from reputable organizations like "Leaping Bunny" or PETA's "Beauty Without Bunnies" to identify cruelty-free products.

Read product labels to verify that they are not tested on animals or do not contain animal-derived ingredients.

Support companies and brands that are committed to cruelty-free practices and sustainable sourcing.

Share information about cruelty-free products with your friends and family, encouraging them to make ethical choices as well.

Consider writing to companies that still engage in animal testing, urging them to adopt cruelty-free practices instead.

By taking these actions, you contribute to reducing animal suffering and promoting ethical treatment and consideration for the well-being of animals on a global scale.

MY NOTES

MY NOTES

CHAPTER SEVENTEEN

Griefwork

LOVING GUIDELINES
WHEN YOUR FRIEND HAS LEFT HIS BODY

ONNECT WITH THE COSMIC ENERGIES:
Begin by finding a quiet and serene space for meditation. Close your eyes, take deep breaths, and envision yourself surrounded by the radiant energy of the cosmos. Feel the presence of the universe and imagine it as a vast, nurturing force. In this state, allow your grief to surface and flow, recognizing it as a natural expression of your love for your departed animal friend. Visualize your animals' spirit merging with the universal energy, becoming a part of a great light. As you meditate, let go of the physical form and embrace the eternal connection you share with your beloved animal companion through the cosmos.

COMMUNICATE THROUGH HEART-CENTERED MEDITATION:
Focus your attention on your heart center and visualize a warm, healing light radiating from within. Imagine your animal friend's essence appearing before you in a gentle, loving form. Engage in a heart-to-heart conversation, expressing your feelings, memories, and gratitude for the time you shared together. Allow

your pet's energy to respond, providing comfort, reassurance, and wisdom. This heart-centered meditation allows you to maintain a profound connection with your animal friend's spirit, fostering healing and closure.

CREATE A MEMORIAL MEDITATION SPACE:

Dedicate a peaceful corner of your home or outdoor space as a memorial meditation area for your departed animal companion. Decorate it with meaningful objects, photographs, or mementos that remind you of your pet. During your meditation sessions, visit this sacred space to commune with your pet's spirit. Sit in stillness, recall fond memories, and send love and gratitude to your beloved animal friend. Imagine their presence and energy surrounding you, offering solace and companionship during your moments of grief. Over time, this memorial meditation space can become a source of comfort and a place to honor your pet's memory.

PRAYERS FOR YOUR ANIMAL FRIEND

Prayers are a way of communication with the source. Here are some prayers of human cultures,
Use whatever feels closest to the feeling you would like to express.

BUDDHISM

"May my beloved [animal friend's name] find peace and liberation from suffering in the realms beyond. May their soul be free from all attachments and experience everlasting happiness and tranquility."

JESUS (ISA) THE PROPHET

"Dear Lord, I entrust the soul of my cherished [animal friend's name] into Your loving care. May they find rest and joy in Your presence, and may I be reunited with them in Your eternal kingdom."

ISLAM

"In the name of Allah, the Most Gracious, the Most Merciful, I pray for the soul of my dear [animal friend's name]. May they find mercy and grace in the hereafter, and may Allah's love surround them for all eternity."

HINDUISM

"O Divine, I offer my prayers for [animal friend's name]. May their soul journey through the cycles of life with ease and find ultimate union with the divine consciousness. Grant them eternal bliss and liberation."

JUDAISM

"Eternal God, I remember and honor the spirit of [animal's name], who brought joy and companionship into my life. May their soul find comfort and rest in Your loving presence, and may their memory be a blessing."

A PRAYER FROM OUR LYRAN CULTURE

"From the cosmic realms, we offer this prayer for our beloved [animal name], who has journeyed beyond the earthly plane. In the light of the Lyran stars, we honor your spirit and the unique energy you brought to this world.

May the celestial energies embrace [animal name]'s soul, guiding them to higher realms of love and understanding. May you find solace in the the one source, where your essence shines eternally.

We thank [animal friend's name] for his/her presence in our lives and for the lessons he/she shared. May their spirit continue to shine brightly, illuminating our hearts with love and connection, across the galaxies.

As we release (animal's name) to the cosmos, may [animal's name] find peace, joy, and eternal harmony among the stars. We remain connected through the universal bond of love, transcending time and space.

In the name of Lyran compassion and unity, we offer our blessings and gratitude. Amen."

MY NOTES

THE 2ND BOOK

YOUR

Star Trek

FUTURE:

LEARNING TO BE, LOVE, AND INTEGRATE

This is a visionary exploration of how the integration of animals as beings with personal rights and the advancements in Artificial Intelligence (AI) is set to transform human-animal communication and contribute to the health and sustainability of the planet.

INTEGRATION OF ANIMALS WITH PERSONAL RIGHTS

Legislation: Increasing legal recognition of animals' sentience will lead to laws that protect their rights and welfare, reducing exploitation and mistreatment.

Education: Educational reforms will instill a sense of stewardship in younger generations, fostering compassionate attitudes toward animals.

Ethical Consumption: A shift toward cruelty-free and sustainable products, including plant-based diets, will reduce the environmental footprint and promote the ethical treatment of animals.

AI'S ROLE IN TRANSFORMING COMMUNICATION

Translating Animal Communication: AI technologies will break down barriers in understanding animal vocalizations and behaviors, allowing for more accurate interpretations of their needs and emotions.

Emotion Recognition: AI will help identify the emotional states of animals, facilitating a more empathetic and responsive interaction.

Augmented Reality Interfaces: AR technologies could enable humans to experience the world from an animal's perspective, fostering deeper empathy and understanding.

Environmental Monitoring: AI tools like sensors and drones will assist in wildlife conservation, aiding in the protection of natural habitats.

Animal-Assisted Therapy: AI-enhanced communication will improve the efficacy of animal-assisted therapy in healthcare settings. It is also important to determine whether the animal is willing to do this based on their free will.

IMPACT ON SUSTAINABILITY AND PLANETARY HEALTH

The convergence of animal rights recognition and AI-driven communication holds great promise for the health of the planet and sustainable living:

Conservation Efforts: Improved understanding and monitoring of wildlife will bolster conservation efforts, ensuring the preservation of biodiversity.

Resource Management: Ethical consumption patterns and respect for animal rights will lead to more sustainable resource use, decreasing the strain on Earth's ecosystems.

Climate Change Mitigation: Shifts toward plant-based diets and ethical consumption reduce the carbon footprint, aiding in the fight against climate change.

Enhanced Ecosystem Health: Protecting animal habitats and recognizing their rights contribute to healthier ecosystems, which are vital for the planet's overall well-being.

In summary, this future envisions a world where humans and animals coexist in a more balanced and harmonious relationship. Through the integration of AI in communication and a societal shift toward recognizing the rights of all sentient beings, we can expect not only an enriched understanding and connection with the animal world but also significant strides in environmental conservation, sustainability, and the overall health of our planet.

THE LIBERATION OF HUMAN KARMA AND FREEDOM FROM REPTILIAN MASTERY

From a multidimensional, loving Lyran perspective, the shift in human-animal communication, combined with increased awareness of animal rights and the incorporation of AI, is essential to the liberation of human karma and the dismantling of reptilian mastery.

Let's explore how these changes are interwoven with the spiritual evolution of humanity:

BREAKING FREE FROM THE KARMIC CYCLE:
Understanding and respecting animals as sentient beings, each with its own consciousness, is a profound step toward healing human karma. The karmic debt accrued from mistreating and exploiting animals has weighed heavily on humanity. Recognizing the intrinsic value of animals helps individuals break free from this karmic cycle. By embracing animal rights and compassionate living, humans generate positive karma. They shift from being oppressors to protectors, and their karmic debts begin to be balanced through acts of kindness and understanding.

EMPATHY AND SPIRITUAL GROWTH:
Engaging in telepathic communication with animals fosters empathy and spiritual growth. When humans can sense the emotions, thoughts, and experiences of animals, they naturally develop a deeper connection to all living beings. Empathy and compassion are integral to spiritual evolution. As humans recognize the interconnectedness of all life forms, they free

themselves from the limitations of ego-driven consciousness, allowing their souls to evolve and expand.

REJECTING REPTILIAN MASTERY:

Reptilian mastery is rooted in the manipulation of human fear, ego, and separation. As individuals awaken to the understanding that animals deserve respect and rights, they begin to question the forces that have perpetuated cruelty and suffering. By rejecting the perpetuation of suffering and understanding that all beings, including animals, have the right to live free from fear and harm, humans undermine the foundations of reptilian mastery. Love, empathy, and unity replace fear and division. Simply by refusing to consume animal-based products, you will feel a change in your frequency, which will allow you to feel and see more and also to receive better with your higher senses.

BALANCING THE LIGHT AND DARK WITHIN:

The recognition of animal rights and the ability to communicate with animals enable humans to embrace their own shadows and transform them into light. This inner transformation helps in breaking free from the reptilian matrix of control, which thrives on human suppression and division. As individuals heal their relationship with animals and the Earth, they also heal themselves, balancing the light and dark aspects of their own souls. This equilibrium further weakens the hold of reptilian forces.

SOWING SEEDS OF LOVE AND UNITY:

The act of communicating with animals with love and respect sends ripples of higher vibrational energy throughout the collective consciousness. These vibrational frequencies of love and unity begin to replace the lower frequencies of fear and control. Each time a human embraces animal rights and demonstrates compassion, they contribute to a collective shift away from reptilian mastery and toward a more harmonious, loving, and unified existence.

In conclusion, the integration of animal rights and AI-assisted communication holds the potential to liberate humanity from karmic bondage and free individuals from reptilian mastery. As humans develop empathy, compassion, and an awareness of the rights of all living beings, they become spiritual warriors in the quest for a more harmonious and enlightened world. The profound transformation in human consciousness, fueled by love and unity, paves the way for humanity to break free from the influence of lower vibrational forces and step into a higher dimension of existence.

BECOMING CONSCIOUS MEMBERS OF THE FEDERATION OF WORLDS:
A MULTIDIMENSIONAL LYRAN PERSPECTIVE

From my viewpoint, the transformation in human-animal communication, the recognition of animal rights, and the integration of AI-assisted communication are integral steps toward humanity becoming respected members of the Federation of Worlds. This is how you can contribute to humanity's elevation on the cosmic stage:

RESPECTING ALL LIFE FORMS:

One of the fundamental principles upheld by the Federation of Worlds is respect for all life forms, regardless of their origins or appearances. As humans shift toward recognizing the rights and consciousness of animals, they align themselves with this universal principle of respect for life. The Federation values societies that are in harmony with their environment and promote the well-being of all sentient beings. By extending this respect to animals, humans demonstrate their readiness to adhere to the Federation's values, which are important if you want to integrate animal rights,

ELEVATING CONSCIOUSNESS:

The transformation in human-animal communication fosters a deeper understanding of the interconnectedness of all life. It raises human consciousness to a level where empathy and compassion are extended beyond their own species. The Federation places great importance on the level of consciousness and unity achieved by a species. When humans awaken to the consciousness of interconnectedness and demonstrate a commitment to the welfare of all life forms, they move closer to being recognized as a spiritually evolved species.

THE ROLE OF AI IN UNIVERSAL COMMUNICATION:

The integration of AI-assisted communication technologies enhances humanity's ability to interact with various alien species. AI acts as a bridge, facilitating the exchange of knowledge, wisdom, and culture between humans and extraterrestrial civilizations. The Federation values the use of technology for peaceful and cooperative purposes. As humans employ AI to foster communication and understanding, they align themselves with the Federation's vision of harmonious interstellar relations.

PROMOTING UNITY AND COLLABORATION:

The Federation seeks members who actively engage in interstellar diplomacy, collaboration, and knowledge sharing. As humans develop the capacity to communicate with multiple species, they demonstrate their commitment to fostering unity and peaceful coexistence.

The ability to interact with various alien species and learn from their experiences is highly regarded by the Federation. It encourages the sharing of knowledge and the development of mutually beneficial relationships.

HEALING AND HARMONY:

The recognition of animal rights and a shift toward compassionate living contribute to the healing of both individuals and the planet. A healed and harmonious society is more likely to be welcomed as a fully active member of the Federation. The Federation values civilizations that actively work toward the betterment of their world and the well-being of their inhabitants. By showing their dedication to healing and harmony, humans take steps toward becoming respected members of this interstellar organization.

In conclusion, the path to becoming respected members of the Federation of Worlds involves aligning human values and behaviors with the principles upheld by this interstellar organization. By respecting all life forms, elevating their consciousness, utilizing AI for universal communication, promoting unity and collaboration, and embracing healing and harmony, humans position themselves as a species ready to take their place in the cosmic community. The journey toward this goal is marked by a deep respect for life, a commitment to unity, and a dedication to peaceful coexistence with all beings, which reflects the values of the Federation of Worlds.

ELEVATING HUMANITY TO THE FEDERATION OF THE WORLDS THROUGH RESPECT FOR ANIMALS

From a perspective that aligns with the Federation of Worlds, humanity's path to becoming respected cosmic members hinges on recognizing and respecting animals as fellow cosmic species. This pivotal transformation involves moving away from a paradigm where animal rights are violated and reflects a departure from mimicking reptilian mastery by consuming animal flesh.

1. RECOGNIZING ANIMALS AS COSMIC SPECIES:

To earn respect among advanced cosmic civilizations, humans must acknowledge that animals are not mere resources for consumption but are cosmic beings with their own rights and place in the universe. This recognition is crucial for aligning with the principles of the Federation of Worlds, which holds all life forms in high regard.

Acknowledging animals as fellow travelers in the cosmos helps humanity transcend its current state of ignorance, marking the first step toward becoming respected members of the Federation.

2. TRANSITIONING AWAY FROM REPTILIAN MASTERY:

Emulating the reptilian mastery involves consuming animals as a way of life. This paradigm is rooted in domination and control over other species, perpetuating suffering and disrespect for life. It hinders humanity's advancement toward cosmic recognition. The shift from this paradigm necessitates a transformation in consciousness, a realization that respect, empathy, and compassion should guide actions toward all life forms. This transition signifies a profound shift toward harmony with the universe.

3. ELEVATING HUMANITY TO COSMIC RESPECT:

By transitioning to a society that respects animal rights, humans elevate themselves to the level where they are seen as worthy members of the Federation of Worlds. This recognition is based on shared values of harmony, respect, and unity with all life forms.

The Federation highly regards civilizations that promote harmony and interconnectedness. Humanity's commitment to end the suffering and exploitation of animals showcases an intention to live in accordance with these cosmic values.

4. PROMOTING PEACEFUL COEXISTENCE:

The Federation seeks societies that actively work toward peaceful coexistence with all beings, both terrestrial and extraterrestrial. Humanity's transition away from the consumption of animal flesh sends a powerful message that they are ready to engage in harmonious relations with fellow cosmic species.

The commitment to non-violence and compassion extends beyond the animal kingdom and showcases humanity's intent to create a more peaceful world. This is an essential aspect of aligning with the Federation's principles.

5. HEALING AND NURTURING THE PLANET:

A society that respects animals fosters a healthier, more balanced relationship with the planet. It promotes ecological stewardship, reducing harm to the environment.

Recognizing that humans are but one of many cosmic species inhabiting the Earth, this approach embraces the healing of both the world and its inhabitants. It sets the stage for a harmonious existence and aligns with the Federation's values of unity and cooperation.

In conclusion, the pathway to earning humanity's place in the Federation of Worlds involves profound changes in the way animals are perceived and treated. By recognizing animals as fellow cosmic species, transitioning away from a reptilian mastery paradigm, elevating their consciousness to cosmic respect, and promoting peaceful coexistence and planet healing, humans can establish themselves as deserving members of the cosmic community. This journey is not just about animal rights; it is about elevating the collective human consciousness toward a state of greater awareness, respect, and interconnectedness with the cosmos.

Afterword

"It is my true pleasure and honor to present you with the above wisdom, and my heart is full of joy that you are finally ready to leave your cocoon and transform into a cosmic butterfly. We have been waiting for you, and now is the time. If you love, love completely; never hold back. Encounter all the wonders of the universe, discover the true essence of your animal friends, their guides, and creators. We love you."

Shen, from the Lyran Galactic Council

Meet

Discover

USEFUL BOOKS:

"Animals in Translation: Using the Mysteries of Autism to Decode Animal Behavior" by Temple Grandin and Catherine Johnson:
Temple Grandin, an accomplished animal scientist and autistic individual, explores the connections between human and animal experiences. She delves into how animals perceive the world, including the role of sensory experiences.

"Our Toxic World: A Guide to Hazardous Substances in Our Everyday Lives" by Doris J. Rapp:
This book provides insights into the impact of environmental toxins, including those related to electromagnetic fields and chemtrails, on human and animal health.

"Pet Food Politics: The Chihuahua in the Coal Mine" by Marion Nestle:
Marion Nestle, a prominent nutritionist and food expert, discusses the politics, marketing, and health implications of commercial pet food, including genetically modified ingredients.

"The Energy Grid: Harmonizing the Earth's Energies" by Maria Wheatley:
This book offers a deeper understanding of Earth's energy grids, ley lines, and their impact on the planet's energy matrix. It may provide insights into how these grids could relate to animal communication.

"The Secret Life of Plants" by Peter Tompkins and Christopher Bird:
While not directly focused on animals, this classic book explores the extraordinary connections between plants and their environment. It underscores the interconnectedness of all living beings.

SYMBOLS THAT SUPPORT TELEPATHIC ANIMAL COMMUNICATION

You can also find great Symbols and Jewelry that will support your spiritual growth and connection on:
www.vegan-cosmic-universe.com

The Om Symbol (ॐ): Om is a sacred sound and spiritual icon in Hinduism, Buddhism, and other spiritual traditions. It is believed to represent the vibration of the universe and can be used as a symbol for connecting with animals on a spiritual level.

The Ankh Symbol (☥): The ankh is an ancient Egyptian symbol that represents life and immortality. Some believe that it can be used to connect with the essence of life in animals and enhance telepathic communication.

The Eye of Horus (𓂀): In ancient Egyptian mythology, the Eye of Horus was considered a symbol of protection, healing, and power. Some people think it enhances one's ability to understand and communicate with animals.

Mandala Symbols: Various mandala symbols can be used for focus and meditation, and they may help individuals enter a more receptive state for telepathic communication.

GEMSTONES THAT SUPPORT YOUR SPIRITUAL EVOLUTION

Lapis Lazuli enhances spiritual insight, intuition, and psychic abilities. It is thought to help deepen telepathic communication with various beings, including animals and benevolent extraterrestrial entities.

Amethyst is known for its calming and protective properties. It may aid in reaching higher states of consciousness and enhancing telepathic abilities, including communication with animals and otherworldly beings.

Labradorite is often associated with enhancing one's intuitive and psychic abilities. It is believed to open the mind to other dimensions, making it easier to communicate telepathically with benevolent entities.

Selenite is considered a powerful crystal for connecting with higher realms and enhancing telepathic abilities. It can help create a clear and open channel for communication with animals and benevolent aliens.

Blue Apatite is thought to stimulate the development of psychic gifts, making it easier to connect with other beings telepathically.

Moonstone: Moonstone is associated with intuition and insight. It may help individuals develop a deeper connection with animals and enhance their telepathic abilities.

Clear Quartz is often used as an amplifier for the properties of other stones. It can enhance your ability to receive and transmit telepathic messages.

Remember, it's essential to cleanse and charge the gemstones before use, and use them as a complementary tool in your telepathic practice. While these gemstones can be used with positive intentions, the true power of telepathic communication comes from your ability to attune to your own intuition and connect with the intended recipients, whether they are animals or benevolent extraterrestrial beings.

ALIEN RACES YOU SHOULD KNOW:

MANTIS RACE (ALIEN MANTIS)

The Mantis race, often referred to as Alien Mantises, is an extraterrestrial species frequently featured in science fiction literature, ufology, and conspiracy theories. These beings are described as humanoid or insectoid, sharing some physical characteristics with Earth's praying mantises, including a slender and elongated body shape, elongated limbs, and large, expressive eyes. The Mantis race is often portrayed as highly intelligent and technologically advanced.

In some accounts and encounters, the Mantis beings are described as benevolent, acting as spiritual guides or protectors of individuals who have experienced contact with them. They are believed to possess profound wisdom and an interest in the spiritual evolution of humanity. However, they often work with grey aliens and, therefore, are not generally benevolent.

ALIEN REPTILIAN RACES
These races are often humanoid or reptile-like beings with a wide range of characteristics and intentions. Just stay away.

DRACONIANS (OR DRACONIDS)
Draconians are a powerful and intelligent reptilian race originating from the Alpha Draconis star system. They are associated with negative intentions, including the manipulation of human affairs and secret control over world governments. They are typically depicted as large, humanoid reptiles with scales and a distinct, often intimidating presence.

REPTOIDS
Reptoids, sometimes referred to as Reptilians, are a hypothetical humanoid reptilian species. They mostly have scaly skin, slitted eyes, and a reptilian appearance. While most modern accounts are malevolent, history proposes a more complex perspective, including possible involvement in ancient Earth civilizations and interactions with humanity.

SIRIANS (OR SIRIAN REPTILIANS)

The Sirian reptilian race is theorized to originate from the Sirius star system. They are a highly advanced and ancient species with various physical forms, including both humanoid and reptilian. In some accounts, they are associated with benevolent intentions and are regarded as protectors of human spiritual development.

LACERTIANS (LIZARD PEOPLE)

Lacertians, or Lizard People, are a humanoid reptilian race often described as inhabiting underground or subterranean areas. They are characterized by their reptilian features and have been subjects of various conspiracy theories. Some narratives suggest that they have influenced human societies and politics.

HUMAN HYBRIDS

Hybrid beings are sometimes depicted as a cross between reptilian and human species. They are often said to possess a blend of physical and mental attributes from both races. Hybrids are sometimes used in covert operations or for specific purposes by the alien reptilian races.

LYRAN ALIEN RACE AND SUB-SPECIES

The Lyran alien race and its associated sub-species are beings often featured in ufology, conspiracy theories, and science fiction literature. These entities originate from the Lyra constellation and have captured the fascination of those who study extraterrestrial phenomena. The Lyran race is depicted with various physical characteristics, sub-species, and intentions.

Here are the primary entities:

1. Lyran Beings

Lyran beings are often humanoid, feline, or feline-humanoid in appearance. They are associated with benevolent intentions and are believed to be protectors and mentors for humanity. Lyran beings are often depicted as wise and spiritually advanced, assisting humans in their evolutionary journey.

2. Vegan (Vega) Beings

Vegan beings are said to originate from the Vega star system in the Lyra constellation. They are depicted as a diverse group of entities, some of whom have humanoid features. Vegan beings are often associated with promoting peace, love, and harmony. They have played a role in the spiritual evolution of Earth.

3. Feline Sub-Species

Within the Lyran race, there are feline sub-species. These entities are characterized by their feline or lion-like features and are believed to possess a strong sense of connection to their own kind and other sentient beings. Feline sub-species are associated with strength, protection, and wisdom.

4. Avian Sub-Species

Originating from the Lyran race, there are avian sub-species that exhibit bird-like characteristics. They are graceful and spiritually enlightened beings who promote healing and transformation.

5. Other Sub-Species

Apart from the feline and avian sub-species, there may be other sub-species within the Lyran race, each with distinct physical and spiritual attributes. These sub-species are often characterized by their diversity and individual roles in assisting humanity.

It's important to emphasize that not everyone who describes himself as Lyran or is in contact with a Lyran is truthful; some humans are also tricked by malevolent beings in disguise, which is very easy. Be careful.

MAY THE LOVE OF THE SOURCE
ALWAYS GUIDE AND PROTECT YOU.

www.ingramcontent.com/pod-product-compliance
Lightning Source LLC
Chambersburg PA
CBHW071957090426
42740CB00011B/1982